THE LEGEND AND BIZARRE CRIMES OF
SPRING HEELED JACK

SPRING-HEEL'D JACK'S DARING LEAP

The first Spring Heeled Jack 'Penny Dreadful' published in the 1840's.

THE LEGEND AND BIZARRE CRIMES OF
SPRING HEELED JACK

PETER HAINING

FREDERICK MULLER LIMITED
LONDON

First published in Great Britain 1977
by Frederick Muller Limited, London NW2 6LE

Copyright © 1977 Peter Haining

ISBN 0 584 10276 3

British Library Cataloguing in Publication Data

Haining, Peter
    The legend and bizarre crimes of Spring Heeled Jack.
    1. Spring Heeled Jack
    1. Title
    364.1'5'0924   HV6248.S/

    ISBN 0-584-10276-3

Printed in Great Britain by
Offset Lithography by Billing & Son Ltd.,
London, Guildford and Worcester

Set in IBM Journal Roman by Tek-Art (Typesetting) Ltd.,
214 Anerley Road, London SE 20

Dedicated to the memory of

TOD SLAUGHTER

(1885-1956)

— who brought Spring Heeled Jack
alive on stage and screen

Contents

Illustrations

'The exploits of Spring Heeled Jack are
still remembered as having frightened
London half out of its wits. The miscreant made night hideous by his tricks
— leaping over hedges to the terror of
lonely pedestrians, waylaying females,
scaring children, and even rendering the
drivers in charge of the mails helpless
with terror. The suburbs of London were
in a far different state forty years ago,
when all this happened, to what they are
now, and it can easily be imagined how
great was the consternation thus occasioned among those residing in them.
People were afraid to venture out after
nightfall. Stories of the wildest and most
extravagant nature got into the newspapers and formed the staple of conversation. By many Spring Heeled Jack was
believed to be a veritable demon; others
declared him to be a nobleman in disguise
who took delight in his cruel sport; while
the majority were in favour of his being
a vulgar footpad, who first terrified those
whom he subsequently plundered. Thus,
while some credited him with horns and
eyes of flame, an opposite set of eye-
witnesses were in favour of a mask and
whitened face; and society was divided
between believers in hoofs, and those
who asserted, with hardly less folly, that
the extraordinary leaps in which he indulged were effected by means of springs
in his boots, powerful enough, some said,
to carry him over houses!'

THE NEWS OF THE WORLD
November 17, 1872

1

The Legend of Spring Heeled Jack

The windows of 'The Green Man' inn were a blaze of lights
and there was the sound of singing and laughter spilling into
the streets of Blackheath as Polly Adams stepped out from a
side door. The attractive young girl hitched her shawl closer
about her shoulders and walked quickly around to the front
of the tall corner building with its picturesque bow windows
and collonaded entrance. For a moment Polly stopped to
glance in the windows, glad that for a couple of hours at least
she would not have to rush backwards and forwards serving
ale and food to the merry-making patrons inside.

It had been a long, busy summer at 'The Green Man', which
was one of the most popular inns on the south side of the
Thames. Conveniently situated as it was just a couple of miles
from the river and the crossing over Greenwich Reach, it
was not surprising that it had become much favoured by
Londoners out for an evening's entertainment. It attracted
both the high and the low, noblemen and countryfolk alike
rubbed shoulders in the low-beamed bars, while serving girls
like Polly bustled from morning to night trying to keep pace
with enormous thirsts and demanding stomachs.

It was hard work, but for Polly, a poor farmer's daughter
from Kent, it was also exciting. Barely seventeen, she was a
pretty, dark-haired girl endowed with a good figure and a

twinkle in her hazel eyes who caught the attention of all but the most drunken customers, and in return for being good-naturedly propositioned and even occasionally man-handled, made a better living than she might have expected on the farm. There was Tom, too — Thomas Evans, the son of the landlord — who had taken a fancy to her. Already they were lovers, stealing time away from their work to make love in Tom's little garret room, where Polly gave herself gladly, proud of her body, the firmness of her full breasts, wide hips and graceful legs. She hoped they would marry eventually, but had asked for nothing, just praying that she would not fall for a child until the time was right. . .

For a moment longer Polly looked towards the inn, half hoping to catch a glimpse of Tom before she set off to the Fair. But there was no sign of him, and she knew that his father would not let him out until much later and probably not until after she herself had returned. Even though the thought of going on her own made her feel just a little bit uneasy, it did not deter her, for she had heard so many stories of this famous event that she just had to see for herself. So with a last glance she turned resolutely towards Blackheath Hill and began to walk.

It was fine and starlit, this night of October 11 1837. Although there was a touch of approaching winter in the air, Polly had decided she only needed a shawl to cover her naked shoulders. Because Mr Evans had only allowed her two hours off to go to the fair, and even that only after much entreating, there had been no time to change and she still wore the blue serving dress and apron of her profession. Although neither cut nor modelled well, the dress could not disguise the trimness of her figure and only enhanced the roundness of her breasts protruding above the laced bodice.

She walked on purposefully, passing little groups of people also making their way up to Blackheath. Occasionally a horse and carriage clip-clopped by on the hard-baked road, and friends acknowledged each other as they met.

The night of October 11 was the second of Blackheath's two big days of the year — May 12 being the other — when the famous 'hog and pleasure' fair, as it was called, was held on the Heath. Dating back to 1683, when it had been

'The Green Man', Blackheath, home of Spring Heeled Jack's victim, Polly Adams.

founded by Lord Dartmouth, it was ostensibly a meeting for the sale of cattle, but instead had became a riotous gathering offering side-shows, entertainments and, perhaps most importantly, drinking.* Men and women of all classes rode or walked from London and the surrounding districts to gape at the shows, ride the entertainments, buy trinkets, rattles and trumpets from the peddlers, spiced gingerbread from the sweetmeat sellers, and drink their fill of ale and spirits. On those two nights of the year Blackheath became a focal point for anyone seeking entertainment — families, lovers, gentlemen and their ladies and hell-raisers of all degrees.

As Polly reached the top of the hill, where it joined with the curiously-named Shooter's Hill Road, she looked away to her left and saw the flickering lights of London and the meandering course of the Thames shimmering in the light of the moon. To her right, as she turned, she could see towards

* In time the Fair became so riotous and notorious that it was suppressed by order of the Government in 1872. Since the early years of this century, however, travelling fairs have been allowed to return to the Heath at Bank Holidays and now draw equally huge crowds from all over South London.

Kent and knew that somewhere out there in the darkness lay her home at Swanley. She had not more than a moment to think of her family, though, for an instant later a shadow fell across her — the shadow of the gallows.

For generations this gallows, and others like it, had stood on the Heath, the bodies of criminals hanging there, rotting, as reminders of the price to be paid for breaking the law. Polly had heard many stories told in 'The Green Man' of bleaching bones having hung for years on these gallows, and she was glad there was not one there now. She shivered slightly and walked on.* Soon the broad expanse of greensward lay in front of her, aptly named because of its bleakness and blackness. On any other night it would not have been a place to venture along, but the lights and noise coming from the multi-coloured stalls and tents which stood on the far side, near the little collection of houses known as Tranquil Vale, relieved the grimness of the place. Polly smiled with anticipation and quickened her stride. To a country girl like her it was all new and exciting, and she had eyes for nothing but the marvels which lay before her.

A few minutes later, joining the crowds who were walking around the swings and roundabouts, the side-shows and stalls, Polly could not conceal her delight at the sights. She wandered down the rows of booths, jostled occasionally by the large, happy crowds. From time to time she stopped to take in something that particularly caught her eye.

In the doorway of one booth stood a pot-bellied man holding aloft a picture of two strange creatures which looked to her like peculiar children.

'Step up,' the man shouted. 'In here are two monstrous children, both alive, having their bellies joined together and embracing one another. Step right up and see for yourselves!'

* The historian George Philipott has written that Shooter's Hill was 'so called for the thievery there practised, where travellers in early times were so much infested with depredations and bloody mischiefs, that order was taken in the sixth year of Richard II, for the enlarging of the highway, according to the statute made in the time of King Edward I, so that they venture still to rob here by prescription.' In 1661, Samuel Pepys passed across the Heath and noted in his diary for April 11, 'Mrs Anne and I rode under the man that hangs upon Shooter's Hill, and a filthy sight it was to see how his flesh is shrunk to his bones.' Despite improvements to the road in 1733, it continued to be a haunt for highwaymen for years thereafter, and even after such men had passed into history, the road retained its evil reputation.

Polly put her hand into the fold of her dress and felt for the precious few coins she had managed to save for this outing. They were so few in number and there seemed to be so many things to see. Perhaps she had better look around everywhere before deciding what to spend her money on.

She went on past a beer stall where several men already lay in a drunken stupor, avoided the insistence of a peddler who pushed some ribbons under her nose, and then came across another stall with the picture of a woman with two heads hanging on the front of it. Before this stood a little group of people listening to a man who was laboriously spelling out the words written below the picture. Polly, who also could not read, joined the group, listening as intently as the others to his words:

'. . . can be seen a woman, 35 years of age, alive, with two heads one above the other; having no hands, fingers, nor toes; yet she can dress or undress, knit, sew, read, sing. This great wonder has been seen by the nobility and. . . '

At that moment Polly felt a hand fall upon her shoulder. As she turned, startled, the hand grasped her shawl and tore it from her shoulders. A cry escaped from her lips and she looked into the grinning face of a man with protruding eyes.

She could tell immediately that he was a nobleman by his appearance, and that of a group of friends standing directly behind him. Her hand flew to her mouth in fright. But before she could move the man had reached forward and taken her by the shoulders. Polly felt a shudder go through her whole body. Her captor's eyes glanced down onto the fullness of her heaving bosom and narrowed perceptibly.

'Sir. . . . ' Polly started as the man's fingers dug into the soft flesh of her shoulders. But at that he pulled her towards him and kissed her hard upon the mouth, smothering her protest. She smelt the brandy on his breath and felt the sweat from his brow rub against her face.

For a moment she was unable to resist. Then, quickly regaining her faculties, she pushed back hard against his chest and broke free from his grip. Immediately she turned and ran blindly away into the crowds, pushing and shoving to get away. The man made no attempt to follow her, but his laughter—a peculiar, ringing laughter—followed her as she ran.

For several moments she ran desparately, then eventually turned a corner and stopped to regain her breath. It was not the first time she had been grabbed by a drunken man, but that usually happened when she was in 'The Green Man', where she half expected such things and knew how to react. Here, however, she had been caught off guard. She realised, too, that in her panic she had fled without her shawl. She sighed unhappily, for it had been a nice one given to her by Tom, but she knew she dare not go back to look for it.

Perhaps it had not been such a good idea to come to the fair on her own after all. Without a man she was obviously at the mercy of any drunk — and now that her shawl had gone, her low-cut dress made her look even more ripe than ever for being molested.

Almost at once the memory of the man with the bulging eyes came flashing back into her consciousness. There had been something weirdly hypnotic about those protruding eyes, something that imprinted them more firmly in her mind than anything else about her attacker. They were something she was never likely to forget. Polly was sure now that her evening was ruined; indeed she would not feel safe until she was back at the inn. She realised she would be sorry that she had not seen any of the exhibits, but then would she be able to concentrate on anything in case that hand fell on her shoulder again?

She paused only a moment longer before making up her mind. And when she set off, not once did she look back. If she had done, she would have seen a small knot of figures following her silently in the gloom.

Polly Adams was almost at the top of Shooter's Hill Road on her way home when the second terrible incident of that night befell her.

By this time she had been walking for some five minutes and her spirits were somewhat restored. However, she was beginning to feel a little cold without her shawl, and already decided to have a glass of mulled ale when she got back to the inn. She wouldn't tell anyone what had happened, though, not even Mr Evans; he would probably have told her she should have gone with the gentleman and let him do what he wanted with her. She might have made some money for herself. But she knew if she allowed that to happen Tom wouldn't want her any more.

It was just as the young girl passed the strange, dark hillock on the heath known as 'Whitefield's Mount' that her reverie was shattered suddenly and terrifyingly. Surrounded by fir trees yet within sight of Shooter's Hill, this gloomy spot had formerly been a butt for artillery practise but had earned its name because of the sermons delivered there by the celebrated preacher, George Whitefield.* Now it was from this humped copse, at first almost completely obscured in the darkness and then dramatically silhouetted against the skyline, that a huge, cloaked figure leapt out and advanced on her with terrible speed.

Polly froze to the spot in an agony of fear. For the second time that night she felt a shiver run up her spine, her heart shot up into her throat, and sweat broke out all over her body. Her mouth fell open, but such was her terror that not a sound came from between her lips.

The figure, appearing gigantic in the shadows, bounded forward towards her on legs that covered such distances at each stride that they hardly seemed human. Behind it swirled a cloak which billowed and flapped noisily. But above this cloak, it was the face which caught and held Polly's attention; a face with eyes that glowed like coals and a mouth which spat flashes of blue fire: a face from the very depths of hell.

Caught like a rabbit in the glare of night lights, the unfortunate girl could not move, could barely force her mind to work. Only the thought that she must be facing the Devil himself raced through her consciousness. Her fear turned to paralysis, she could not even seek the escape of fainting to black out this terrible vision.

A moment more and the figure was upon her. With a final leap that carried the creature almost over her and indeed blotted out everything except his frightful shape, he confronted her. There was the smell of sulphur and the warmth of fire on Polly's face and in her nostrils. But she could not

---

* Writing of this spot in his diary for March 16, 1687, John Evelyn commented, 'I saw a trial of those devilish, murdering, mischief-doing engines called bombs, shot out of a mortar-piece on Blackheath. The distance that they are cast, the destruction which they make where they fall, is prodigious.'

blink or swallow. The eyes which glared at her seemed to swim in flame, and when the creature breathed, blue fire flashed from between his lips.

She could tell now that it was a man; but what kind of devil man? What kind of being to leap out of the night like that? She stared transfixed as the creature lifted its arms and for the second time that evening fingers grabbed her naked shoulders.

At that moment the first cry escaped from her lips. For the fingers that clutched her soft, fair skin were cold and hard like iron. They dug into the flesh savagely, breaking the skin, causing blood to flow.

The face moved closer to hers, the fire warm against her cheek. The gall rose in her throat, choking her cry, causing her to stagger backwards. But for the iron fingers on her shoulders she would certainly have fallen.

A laugh rang out from the creature. A peculiar, ringing laughter, a laugh which, as she was to recall later, she had heard before that evening. The eyes flashed again and she saw they were distended from their sockets, protruding to such a degree that she could see the white of the iris around the dark, menacing spots of the pupils. These eyes, too, she had already seen not so long ago.

At that moment the man released his grip on her and the agony of his clasp eased her shoulders a little. A wave of nausea came over her and she would have fallen this time for sure if his hands had not grasped the front of her dress.

Polly felt her knees begin to buckle and then she was lifted almost off her feet as the man's hands seized either side of her bodice and tore the strings apart. In a moment her dress was shredded to the waist, her breasts thrown open and her skin felt the chill of the night air. She gasped with pain and horror.

The figure tore at her garments again, wrenching the bodice completely from her body. The blue serving dress was hauled down over her thighs. The iron-like fingers dug savagely into the flesh of her waist, scratching down across her exposed stomach and leaving angry weals across her white skin.

At last a full scream broke from her lips. She tried weakly

to cover her breasts with one arm and her other hand moved down between her thighs. She was almost naked now, almost unconscious with the horror of the ravishing.

As suddenly as he had begun, the man stopped his attack. For a moment he seemed to stand back to look at his handiwork as the young girl began to slide slowly down into the remnants of her torn and shredded clothes. A moan that was half-sob and half-cry broke from her again, and for a last time she managed to raise her face to look upon her attacker.

The creature stepped back, hands on hips; another flash of fire illuminating his terrible face; another ringing laugh escaping from his lips.

Polly could hold herself up no longer and finally fell back, momentarily feeling the dampness and cold of the grass against her exposed body. Her eyes rolled in her head; if the creature was about to rape her, she knew in her failing consciousness that she would not be able to resist. . .

But as oblivion mercifully claimed the stricken young woman, her strange assailant had already turned his back on her and was speeding away with huge, bounding steps into the night.

The infamous Spring Heeled Jack was on his way into the annals of crime and destined to become a legend that has baffled, mystified and fascinated people from that day to this.

The name, or as it is sometimes used as a descriptive term, Spring Heeled Jack, is familiar to most adults and a great many children, not only in the British Isles but in a good many foreign countries too. It has become, like many a catch-phrase or saying, an expression whose origins are no doubt obscure to most people — more than likely unknown — but quite precise in its definition.

I have only to take down the *Chamber's Twentieth Century Dictionary* from the shelf in my study to find an immediate and simple definition:

> SPRING HEELED, having springs on one's heels, as SPRING HEELED JACK, supposed to do great leaps and play pranks or commit robberies.

9

On the same page, I find a variation of this, which helps explain (as we shall see later) how our central character's name has varied in certain districts of the country:

SPRING'AL, SPRING'ALD, an active springy young man, a youth.

My *Oxford Dictionary* also elaborates a little further on the point thus:

SPRING HEELED JACK — a name given to a person who from his great activity in running or jumping, especially in order to rob or frighten people, was supposed to have springs in the heels of his boots. *dial.* a highwayman.

We can see from these definitions how the title has become such a standard part of our vocabulary even if, as I said, its real origins are scarcely considered. For we all know, or have seen, the boy or young man who moves especially lightly on his feet or is particularly agile when it comes to jumping, and consequently is referred to as a 'Spring Heeled Jack'.

As a schoolboy in Middlesex there was a classmate of mine who earned a considerable reputation for jumping ditches (or 'dags' as we used to call them) that no-one else would tackle. Lead him to any small pond or stream and challenge him to cross it at a bound, and without a second thought for his safety over he would go on feet that seemed to have wings. I never once saw him fall in or even stumble, which was just as well for I am sure he would have been in for a terrible time from his mother if he had! In any event, he was nicknamed 'Spring Heeled Jack' — though his name was Paul and his favourite footwear was plimsolls.

'Spring Heeled' Paul has his counterpart wherever you care to go, and on a visit to America only a year or so back, I heard one of that country's leading high jumpers described by a sophisticated New Yorker as 'just like a spring-heeled jumping jack'. The man had no idea why that phrase should have come into his mind when he sought a term to describe the feats of the athlete in question; it was just something he had picked up as a child. He was even more amazed when I told him a little of the term's origin in the bizarre legend of

Spring Heeled Jack.

And it is this strange, virtually forgotten, and certainly never before fully-documented legend that we shall be considering in this book. It is an unusual and at times macabre story, dealing with a criminal who adopted perhaps the strangest 'disguise' in the annals of crime, and whose name has outlived him when those of so many other criminals have gone with them to the grave.

It is a story made all the stranger by the fact that the identity of the man who played this role was not revealed at the time, and it is only now, in this book, that we can be anything like certain who that mysterious first Spring Heeled Jack was. I say 'first' advisedly, for there are reports of criminal activities answering this description stretching from the first half of the nineteenth century to just before the Second World War! Such longevity is hardly possible for a single individual, so we can be certain that the name of the leaping villain was employed by several subsequent persons who no doubt counted on his fearsome reputation generating the necessary fear in victims to enable a crime to be carried out with the minimum of opposition!

Let me quote you one example of an attack by Spring Heeled Jack on a young woman taken from *The Graphic* of August 1876 to show you what I mean:

> Out of the darkness sprang a huge, cloaked figure. In an instant the man had thrown aside his cloak, revealing a hideous and frightful appearance. Blue and white flames vomited from his mouth, and his eyes appeared like balls of fire. The young girl who witnessed all this was so terrified that she fainted right away.

This is a report made almost forty years after Spring Heeled Jack had first appeared. Yet as the report goes on to say, 'when revived, the young maiden had no doubt but that she had come face to face with the terror known as "Spring Heeled Jack".'

It was when I first read reports such as this — which I had looked up as a result of hearing oral tales about this legendary criminal — that I began to wonder why no detailed study had ever been made of a figure who for over a century

11

and a half had survived in public memory; a man who for a time was responsible for holding large sections of the British population in a grip of terror, who was later to become the 'hero' of literature and plays, and who gave his name and reputation to our very language.

Here, I thought, was a figure who, in his day, attracted the same kind of comment and newspaper reportage as the notorious Jack the Ripper — yet while the Ripper had over the years been the subject of book after book, poor Jack was left to moulder in the files and records. It seemed a sad error to me, all the more so because his history would surely be of interest to anyone who had ever uttered his name in another context and wondered, albeit for just a moment, where it might have come from.

I examined, first, what little I knew of the story.

I had first heard the name used, as I mentioned, at school; but the realisation that it described a notorious criminal who made a speciality of sensational exploits had not come until, as an adult, I heard my first story of his activities in Essex.

While researching a quite different subject, an old lady in Colchester, a district where I was living, told me how, as a child, she remembered the neighbourhood being a hot-bed of rumours about a strange character called Spring Heeled Jack. Naturally being interested, I asked her what she knew of this man. She said that apparently he had been up to his leaping activities in the vicinity of the Army Barracks. (Colchester, which is noted as the 'Oldest Recorded Town in Britain', has been an army garrison for many years, and through its gates soldiers have been despatched to trouble spots around the world, and still are today — mostly to Northern Ireland).

It seemed that a masked and cloaked figure with flashing eyes had bounded through the barracks one evening while a platoon of soldiers was being assembled for urgent departure abroad. The leaping man had allegedly thrown the troops into a panic and they had all fled from the parade ground as fast as their legs would carry them — Sergeant Major, officers and all!

Of course, said the old lady, the Army had tried to hush the story up. It was not a good thing to have it thought that soldiers of Queen Victoria — men who had helped establish

12

an empire on which, it was claimed, the sun would never set — had bolted from a solitary man; even a fire-breathing, agile figure like Spring Heeled Jack! But such were the facts as she had heard them — and she believed that there were stories about this person that went back well into the early part of the nineteenth century.

Had she ever heard of any arrest being made of this terrifier of soldiers? No, she had not, and she was sure that not only had he never been caught; despite the most extensive searches and operations carried out to apprehend him; but that no one had any real idea who he might be.

It was a fascinating story, and I was only sorry that the old lady's memory could not provide any further clues.*

A little follow-up research on this intriguing introduction to the legend, however, soon convinced me I was on the track of a unique tale of crime. I found that during the period of his major reign of terror, this strange figure who leapt on unwary travellers, attacked young girls and women, delighted in halting mail coaches by terrifying the drivers — and may even have been responsible for murder — attracted as many headlines and alarmed the authorities as much as his later compatriot, Jack the Ripper.

I learned that from the late 1830's onwards he confounded the authorities, outwitted all attempts to catch him (including those of policemen, vigilantes and whole battalions of troops specially drafted in for the man-hunt and no doubt hoping to restore some of their service's hurt pride!) and even boldly confronted soldiers brave enough to challenge him. These he reportedly 'slapped across the face with his ice cold hands' before disappearing into the darkness with his eerie laugh ringing behind him.

There was obviously no denying from accounts like these that he was a highly dramatic figure — if also a very dangerous one. Who had first coined his name, it seemed impossible to tell, but there was no question that he earned it with his

---

* There is, however, a little more information to be found on this story in the Reverend E. Cobham Brewer's work, *The Reader's Handbook.* Under an entry for 'Spring Heeled Jack' it is stated, 'Even so late as 1877-8 an officer in Her Majesty's service caused much excitement in the garrisons stationed at Aldershot, Colchester and elsewhere by his "spring-heel" pranks.' We shall be returning to these incidents again later in the book.

amazing leaps as he sped from the scene of his crimes or away from his persuers — springing over men on horseback, high garden walls and even small buildings.

I was intrigued to learn that those who had encountered him — and retained enough of their faculties — swore that he had concealed iron springs in his tall leather boots and he used these to effect his leaps. Some said he had the appearance of a devil with eyes like balls of fire and a mouth that vomited flames; others that his face was whitened like a corpse and partly covered by a silver mask. Another opinion maintained he had terrible claws instead of nails and his cloak could be miraculously stretched out rigid and used like a glider wing to jump from balconies or buildings.

Darker tales still said he was half-man, half-supernatural being who had horns protruding from his forehead. There was talk that his feet were actually cloven and that he left prints like horse-shoes in the mud. It was also asserted that no weapon could hurt him and that, like a vampire, he could only be killed by a round, silver bullet. And when he sped off into the night with the cry, 'The day is yours — leave the night to me!' his feet made a dull, thudding sound that seemed to echo through the very earth.*

In the West of England, I was told, nurses used his name to frighten children. In the South he was believed to be a foot-pad out to rob people after he had terrified them with his disguise — although there was not a scrap of evidence he had ever taken a penny from anyone. Inquiries into the allegations that he had robbed people lead to the conclusion that

---

* In her fascinating study of Highwaymen, *Stand & Deliver* (1928) historian Elizabeth Villiers devotes some attention to the legend of Spring Heeled Jack and comments on this aspect: "A thousand tales were afloat and all lost nothing in the telling. Plenty of people definitely swore they had seen him leap right over the roofs of large houses, the cottages and hayricks were as nothing to him, the mail coaches and post chaises and family barouches were taken in his stride. Then, rather unaccountably, public opinion veered from thinking him a new form of highwayman and declared he was an inventor experimenting with a form of flying machine, while others maintained he was not flesh and blood but a haunting spirit." Miss Villiers also makes the interesting point that the theory the attacker was a ghost persisted in some quarters despite the sworn statements of the women who had been assaulted. She concedes, though, that there might be an element of doubt in those who said Jack only kissed them because "the kisses might have existed in their imagination, and the Psychical Research Society has records of 'elementals' who haunt scenes of crime and who — according to these investigators — behave in much the same way as did Spring Heeled Jack."

victims might have been holding coins or carrying purses at the moment of attack and dropped these in their panic, but there was nothing to say Jack was directly responsible for the loss. Indeed in Wales, he was not considered an evil-doer at all, but a kind of Robin Hood figure who took pheasants, hares and even lambs from the gentry and left them on the doorsteps of the poor.

The story did not end there, either. Such a man could not remain the province of gossip and the newspapers for long. Soon he was the 'hero' of 'Penny Dreadful' weekly serials — his exploits made still more incredible and alarming. In time, too, he became a star of Victorian melodrama: there were several plays based on his adventures and staged with enormous success at the small theatres and 'gaffs' of London and the provincial cities. Later still, he even attracted the early film-makers, and there remains one picture which utilised elements of his story. (What a possibility he also obviously offers to modern film companies who are always so eagerly searching for fresh material!).

At this point I needed no further convincing that here was a story worth the telling. A unique story from an age redolent with crime and passion, when enormous gulfs existed between the rich and the poor, the nobility and the working class. For here was a figure who cocked a snook at society and ran the most appalling risks — to have been caught would have meant death at the end of a rope without any shadow of doubt — yet whose identity went with him to the grave.

I determined to go back into the dusty archives of our national newspapers and dig out details of those of Spring Heeled Jack's appearances which had been reported. I set myself the task of tracing his influence both on his times, and on the literature and mediums of entertainment which subsequently helped build up his legend. I wanted, too, to examine the theories and ideas that had been put forward about him over the intervening years. Most of all I wanted to try and see if, once and for all, I could unmask the man who was Spring Heeled Jack, especially if there might be some truth in the suggestion that he had been a famous eccentric nobleman!

The result of my enquiries now forms this book. From the first vague rumours of his existence back in 1837 to the seriously advanced suggestion made in 1961 that he was not a human being at all but a man from space, I have tried to trace the 'Legend and Bizarre Crimes of Spring Heeled Jack' as my title states. I trust that for the reader to whom the term is just one that comes to mind when thinking of someone who jumps well, it will prove as revealing in the reading as it did to me in the researching and writing.

In his otherwise outstanding and painstaking book, *The Victorian Underworld*, (1970) historian Kellow Chesney discusses how simple Victorian servants were sometimes duped by the cunning of the criminal classes who preyed on the better-off homes of London. 'Perhaps very unwillingly,' he writes 'they would cover up the criminals' tracks, and many of the improbable exploits of thieves like Spring Heeled Jack may have begun with servants hard pressed for a story. (Jack himself was a pure legend.)'

Much as I am loathe to dispute the findings of a fellow author I am afraid he is wrong. Spring Heeled Jack was certainly not 'pure legend'. He *did* exist — and exist with a vengeance as we shall see. . .

2

'A Ghost, Bear or Devil?'

England, in the late 1830's, was on the verge of the greatest period of development that it had known in its history. With the accession of the young Queen Victoria in 1837, there began an era of unprecedented and constant change in economic circumstances, social custom and intellectual atmosphere that was to leave a mark on the very fabric of the nation and give a special meaning to the expression the 'Victorian Age'.

From this date to the end of the century the period was to be marked by the fact that there was no great war or fear of catastrophe from abroad, and the people themselves developed powers of self-discipline and self-reliance which were the basis of so many of their achievements. The emergence of the steam railway alone; spreading its tentacles from one end of the land to the other with amazing rapidity; was a herald of many later innovations in transport and communications.

But it was also a time when there were great differences in the circumstances of the people; when the rich and powerful enjoyed almost limitless freedom and the poor seemed sunk in the slough of poverty and despair. As industrial expansion went on furiously so did the demand for labour; and with this the heartless exploitation by the minority of business owners and landlords of the majority of working people, who were heaped into cramped and unhealthy slums, worked half to death and paid wages that barely kept them above starvation level.

And despite the high moral tone adopted by its so-called respectable citizens, the era was one when vice flourished as never before, with terrible abuses practised on women, children and young girls in particular. Of course women as a group were reduced to a position of subjugation which has been rightly described as almost Muslim in its standards of contempt. Men, by contrast, were expected to be 'manly' and all manner of scurrility by the male, of both high or low estate, was excused under this name.

Writers such as Charles Dickens and Henry Mayhew have provided us with the most graphic pictures of this age, covering the entire spectrum of public life from the slums to the great houses. They have also shown us, with especial care lavished on the details, the workings of the large and diverse underworld of London. Historian Kellow Chesney has succinctly expressed the information they offer thus:

> In London. . . there were examples of almost every kind of criminal refuge and breeding ground, from crazy, piled up tenements that had been villainous under Queen Anne to the squalid new warrens of the industrial age. As in every great city, the criminal community, for all its diversity, remained firmly attached to its citadels. The master cracksman or swell pickpocket might live in a respectable suburb like Camden Town or New Cross, but it was through contacts in Snow Hill, Whitechapel or the Old Mint that he found his associates and the means of carrying on his trade. In lodging house kitchens, in the tap-rooms of flash pubs, in coffee shops and eating houses, among festoons of second-hand clothes in little grotto-like shops off the reeking hubbub of Rosemary Lane, was carried on the essential traffic of the underworld. Here robberies were hatched, the disposal of stolen property arranged, packets of counterfeit money marketed, forged documents commissioned, and above all, information bought and exchanged. Deep inside the rookery the coiner carried on his elaborate craft in relative security and the hunted thief went to ground.

The fact that some kind of order was established over this lawlessness was due in no small measure to the appearance of the frockcoated and tophatted 'Peeler'.

CHRONICLE.

June 25, 1837.   Price 3½d.

Proclamation at Temple Bar
OF HER MOST GRACIOUS MAJESTY QUEEN ALEXANDRINA VICTORIA I.

William and Mary were the first of the sovereigns of England proclaimed at the present structure—Temple Bar—(a representation of which we have given above) which took place on the sixteenth of February, 1689, and which ceremony has been substantially preserved ever since. Prior to the year 1670, near the site of this only remaining city gate, were placed posts and chains only, as the western barrier of the city. Before the building of the gate, the kings were proclaimed, in solemn state, attended by a great retinue of officers and civil authorities, at West Cheap, near Saint Paul's Cross, which stood opposite to the end of Wood-street, at the corner of which proclamation is made at this time. The ceremony, so far as a pageant is exhibited, was, prior to the proclamation of William and Mary, a matter of great splendour. The Lord Mayor, bare headed, as the king's lieutenant, delivered the sword of state to the sovereign, which was returned to him with a speech from the kings or queens of that period, dictated according to their respective notions of princely supremacy and regal authority; the various city companies, in state liveries, and all the insignia of their respective crafts, being present. It sometimes happened that the citizens left the scene with fears for the maintenance of their chartered rights, at other times elated with joy from an assurance of their augmentation. It is difficult to obtain very accurate authority touching these proclamations; great research is necessary, and the destruction of some of the city books by fire increases the difficulty. After the great fire of London, in the year 1666, Temple Bar offered an object for the exercise of the abilities of Sir Christopher Wren. The centre is a broad gateway, and the sides are furnished with posterns for foot passengers; the whole is constructed of Portland stone, of the Corinthian example. On the eastern side, two niches contain the statues of Queen Elizabeth and James the First, with the arms of England over the key-stone. On the west side, are statues of Charles the First and Charles the Second, in Roman habits; they were executed by Bushnel. On the east side, was an inscription, nearly obliterated, to the following purport: " Erected in the year 1670, Sir Samuel Starling, Mayor; continued in the year 1671, Sir Richard Ford, Lord Mayor; and finished in the year 1672, Sir George Waterman, Mayor.

A London newspaper at the time of the accession of Queen Victoria.

The formation of a police force in London had followed as a direct result from Sir Robert Peel's Metropolitan Police Act of 1829. Although there had been some opposition to the idea of the force — there were people who believed they would act as spies and actually create crime — once organised under two Commissioners it became noticeably effective in the battle against it.

Not surprisingly the members of the force were intensely disliked by the poor and criminal classes of London, and found it advisable always to travel in groups of at least two. After operating successfully in London for some years — and occasionally being called into the provinces to deal with specific problems — the force was expanded in 1835 by the Municipal Reform Act. Thereafter most large towns and cities soon had groups of 'Peelers' of their own.

Another result of the birth of this police force was to cause the more determined and daring criminals to move from place to place in search of fresh pickings — and to keep ahead of the law. They also hoped that such mobility might make difficulties for the authorities if they were caught and it proved hard to establish under exactly whose jurisdiction they came. In effect, there was emerging a new type of criminal.

And it was against this background that the man who was to become known as Spring Heeled Jack first made his appearance . . .

A cold, wintry sunlight shone on the grey Portland stone edifice of London's Mansion House as the activities of the day began to stir around this hub of the city's life. It was the morning of Monday, January 9 1838, and for those London folk who had time to stop for a few words with friends they met, it was the first day they could remember since well before Christmas when the sun had actually shone.

Everyone was still heavily wrapped up against the cold, but at least the pale shafts of sunlight falling on the cobbled streets gave a little relief from what had been a terrible winter.

The few ladies to be seen about at this hour were in heavy

gowns and fur bonnets and had their hands thrust deeply into muffs, while their top-hatted gentlemen companions were sporting the long, multi-coloured mufflers, wrapped voluminously around their necks and which had become fashionable, as well as necessary, during the cold, dark days. Those street sellers, work-bound citizens and grubby urchins who were not so fortunate, could only blow on their hands and quicken their steps to keep warm. Perhaps hardest-hit of all were the drivers of coaches and horse-drawn commercial vehicles who had no alternative but to tend to their reins at the expense of their red hands and pinched faces.

For all these citizens, though, the sunlight brought a little respite, and many of them soothed themselves with the thought that at least the low temperature had not brought the terrible snows of Christmas Day two years previously when 'The Great Snow' had isolated London for two days. At that time, mail coaches had been overwhelmed by the driving snowstorm, houses engulfed and all business had been brought to a standstill, but the Christmas just passed had exposed the population to heavy frosts instead of snow. Most lakes and rivers, and even parts of the Thames had frozen, and there were many accidents both in homes and outside. The old, particularly, had been hard hit, and the death toll was already over the 100 mark in the London district for that month alone.

The weather was, as always, the main topic of conversation, but the newspapers had already passed on to other matters, and the front pages that Monday morning were discussing the Anti-Poor Law meetings taking place throughout the country, and taking a slightly superior attitude to a report just published from Portugal about the 'daring bands of robbers who render travelling (unless strongly escorted) both dangerous and difficult'. In less than eight months, it was stated, there had been 1,442 murders and 329 robberies on the roads of that country. There was nothing the British Press enjoyed more than showing how even our allies did not yet enjoy the same standards of law and order as ourselves!

It was plain, though, that throughout all the discomforts of the winter, life in London had continued to run its normal course. And this morning at the Mansion House was to be no

The Mansion House in 1838.

different as the Lord Mayor conducted his usual Monday session to hear matters of concern to his citizens.

Already small groups of people were hurrying up the stone ballustraded staircase. Above them, caught in the sunlight, was the bas-relief of the lady representing London, attended by the other figures of Liberty, Commerce and the River Thames. Once inside, they walked slowly and quietly to the Common Hall where the Lord Mayor would hold audience from ten o'clock to twelve. As Chief Magistrate of the metropolis he possessed the power to settle disputes and dispense justice with the full weight of the law behind him.

At precisely ten o'clock, the ushers called for silence in the Common Hall, and as soon as a hush had fallen over the crowd, a small group of liverymen, lead by the sword and mace-bearers proceeded into the hall. Behind them walked the grey-wigged, imposing figure of the Lord Mayor, Alderman Sir John Cowan.

Sir John, in his violet silk robe, furred and bordered with black velvet, and gold chain, was a tall, kindly-looking man, already well-liked by the citizens of London despite having served only two months in office. Although benevolent by nature, this member of the Waxchandlers Livery Company was still a firm believer in discipline and used the full rigours of the law when the need arose. For his long service to the City as a sheriff, and excellence in his profession, as a wax chandler, he had been made a Baronet in the previous November.

Accompanied by the Recorder, the Common Sergeant, the four City Pleaders and the City Solicitor, Sir John took his seat at the head of the Hall. For a moment or more there was the sound of the audience settling itself, and then the session began.

The formal business came first; applications from traders and businessmen, some simple disputes that required settling and a report of plans for some rebuilding in the city. The Lord Mayor quietly nodded his assent or disapproval after the Recorder had presented each case and summoned the appropriate witnesses. For the best part of an hour and a half the proceedings continued in their time-honoured way: there was little to differentiate this Monday morning from any other.

It was when the Recorder announced that, for his part, he had completed the business of the day, that the Lord Mayor raised himself up slightly in his seat, and took out a sheet of paper from a small folder lying on the table before him. For a moment he was silent, then he held the paper up slightly in front of him. The crowd, whose attention had been drifting with the passage of time, suddenly found themselves drawn to Sir John with renewed interest.

'A short while ago,' he began in a low, serious voice, 'I received a letter upon a subject, the odd nature of which, induced me to withhold it from the public for some days in the expectation that some statement might be made through a source of indisputable authority relative to the matter of which it treats. However, nothing having materialised, I believe it is only right and proper that its contents should now be revealed to common notice.'

The Lord Mayor indicated to the Recorder and held out the paper. 'The Recorder will now read out its contents.'

A silence fell over the audience as faces turned in puzzlement from one to another. At the special bench set aside for the newspaper reporters, the group of men began to show their first real interest in the morning's proceedings.

The Recorder cleared his throat and started to read:

> To the Right Honourable, the Lord Mayor. My Lord — The writer presumes that your Lordship will kindly overlook the liberty he has taken in addressing a few lines on a subject which within the last few weeks has caused much alarming sensation in the neighbouring villages within three or four miles of London.
>
> It appears that some individuals (of, as the writer believes, the highest ranks of life) have laid a wager with a mischievous and foolhardy companion (name as yet unknown), that he durst not take upon himself the task of visiting many of the villages near London in three different disguises — a ghost, a bear and a devil; and moreover, that he will not enter a gentleman's gardens for the purpose of alarming the inmates of the house. The wager has, however, been accepted, and the unmanly villain has succeeded in depriving seven ladies of their senses.

At this point murmurs of surprise went up from the audience and conversations began to break out all over the Hall. The reporters were now scribbling feverishly and one man who had fallen behind in his copying was urging his neighbour to give him the full text. The Lord Mayor half raised his hand and at this the Common Sergeant called for silence again. When the noise had subsided, the Recorder began to read once more.

> At one house the man rang the bell, and on the servant coming to the open door, this worse than brute stood in no less dreadful figure than a spectre clad most perfectly. The consequence was that the poor girl immediately swooned, and has never from that moment been in her senses, but on seeing any man, screams out most violently, 'Take him away!'
>
> There are also two ladies (which your Lordship will regret to hear), who have husbands and children, and who are not expected to recover, but likely to become burdens to their families.
>
> For fear that your Lordship might imagine that the writer exaggerates, he will refrain from mentioning other cases, if anything more melancholy than those he has already related.
>
> The affair has now been going on for some time, and, strange to say, the papers are still silent on the subject. The writer is very unwilling to be unjust towards any man, but he has reason to believe

that they have the whole history at their finger ends, but, through interested motives, are induced to remain silent.

It is, however, high time that such a detestable nuisance should be put a stop to, and the writer feels assured that your Lordship, as the chief magistrate of London, will take great pleasure in exerting your power to bring the villain to justice.

Hoping your Lordship will pardon the liberty I have taken in writing, I remain your Lordship's most humble servant.

Immediately the Common Hall became a hub-bub of exclamations and conversation. Only those at the front of the crowd heard the Recorder conclude with the name of the writer of the amazing letter, 'A Resident of Peckham'.

Again the Common Sergeant called for order. When at last silence fell, all eyes were turned to the Lord Mayor.

Sir John took the letter back from the Recorder as it was handed up to him, and, glancing at it briefly, spoke once more.

'On first reading this letter I observed to myself, as our friends on the other side of the Atlantic are in the habit of saying it is "extraordinary if true".' The hint of a smile crossed his features. Did he believe it was a hoax or a practical joke, the crowd wondered?

'In my opinion,' he went on, as if answering the unasked questions, 'it is not calculated for the meridian of London, but if any trick has been practised by fools, I have no doubt that the vigilance of the police can be depended upon to prevent annoyance.

'It appears to me that the letter, which is written in a very beautiful hand, is the production of a lady, who might have been terrified by some bugaboo into this mode of obtaining retribution at the hands of the Lord Mayor. However,' he added somewhat firmly, 'as this terrible vision has not entered the city, I cannot take cognizance of its iniquities.'

The faces of the audience began to register confusion at these words. It was difficult to tell if the Lord Mayor believed the story or not. To some, it seemed all too likely in these days when all manner of footpads and robbers were abroad. Even the most sceptical felt there was probably a germ of truth in the story.

Just as the hub-bub was about to begin again, a man sitting near the front of the crowd rose slowly to his feet. He was a well-dressed aristocratic-looking gentleman and seeing him standing the Recorder enquired if he wished to speak on the matter of the letter. The man nodded his head slightly.

'If your Lordship pleases,' he began slowly, 'I have heard tell that the servant girls about Kensington, Hammersmith and Ealing tell dreadful stories of this ghost or devil.' He hesitated a moment and then continued with conviction in his voice: 'I have myself spoken with a blacksmith whom this fellow attacked on one occasion. The unfortunate man was beaten and had his flesh torn with iron claws. The creature is also said to tear the clothes off the backs of females.'

He added 'However, not one of the injured people has been known to tell their story. Perhaps they didn't like to tell it for fear of the ridicule it might bring upon them.'

At this, the man sat down obviously having said all he was going to. Both the Recorder and Lord Mayor looked around the Hall to see if anyone else might add further information. The low chatter continued, but no one stood up.

Sir John was obviously still far from convinced of the danger of what he saw as exaggerated pranks. But he was not a man to make hasty judgements. Perhaps with time the matter might resolve itself.

'It is my belief,' he summed up, 'that one of the ladies who has lost her senses is my correspondent. Perhaps I might hope that she will do me the favour of a call, and I will then have an opportunity of getting from her such a description of the demon as would enable me to catch him, in spite of the paid press and police!'

With another half-smile, the Lord Mayor rose from his chair and, followed by his entourage, strode from the room. Immediately he had left there was a jostle of people to leave the room and head for the streets. Here was a rare new piece of gossip — a demon attacker loose in London!

At the head of this buzzing crowd were the reporters — they had a real mystery story to get to their editors.

The story of the 'Ghost, Bear or Devil' that was said to be terrorising the citizens in the vicinity of the capital appeared in all the national newspapers the following morning, Tuesday January 10th. It was an age when even the most dramatic piece of news warranted no more than a single column headline — and then usually of the most prosaic nature — but nonetheless the story found a prominent position in most journals, and even the illustrious and sober-minded *Times* placed it close to its main leader on the centre pages.

The Times in fact devoted nearly half a column to the events at the Mansion House, but strongly rebuffed the suggestion that it, or any of its contemporaries, were 'paid press' and had suppressed the story of the attacker because he might be a nobleman.

In both the press and in the streets there was much speculation as to who the letter writer, the mysterious 'Resident of Peckham', might be. Some were inclined to agree with the Lord Mayor — who had, after all, examined the actual letter — that the writer was one of the ladies who had 'lost her senses', and the matter should be treated with some scepticism. Others, however, felt the style was more in keeping with a man, perhaps disguising his handwriting. Everyone, press and people, believed that it was a story which should be fully investigated.

As might have been expected, London became a hot-bed of rumour throughout the day. There was hardly a public house to be found where someone was not recounting an experience with this devilish assailant. Many a servant girl in Kensington, Hammersmith and Ealing boasted to her friends that she had been one of the young women to have seen the monster. 'And what a terror he was, with eyes like the devil and hands ready to tear the life from you!'

There were scattered reports, too, that the creature had actually been seen — in locations widely separated on either side of the Thames and mostly at precisely the same time. The 'bugaboo' was certainly a man of extraordinary abilities!

By evening, the rumours had caught such a hold on the more superstitious that the streets of London were unusually quiet. The theatres, gaffs and public houses noted quite a decline in the numbers of common men and women who

were about, although to the swells and their ladies the matter
was rather 'droll' and some even set out in their carriages to
the designated locations in the hope of seeing the demon.

But fact or fiction, prank or not, the story had caught
London's imagination, and the following morning, crowds
were already beginning to assemble around the Mansion
House from first light. If there were to be any further developments in the story, it was believed they would surely
be revealed by the Lord Mayor at his morning session.
Queues soon began to form with great speed.

By the time admission was being made to the Common
Hall, a crowd of over 1,000 people had assembled outside the
building, and the ushers were having to restrict admission as
best they could. There was no need for anyone to ask what
had generated all the interest.

The Lord Mayor and his retinue appeared promptly at ten
o'clock, Sir John already having been informed of the packed
crowd in the Hall and the many more who had been denied
entrance and were still outside.

Sir John knew that it would be pointless to observe the
usual procedure for business and decided to come straight to
the matter of the mysterious attacks. There was not a soul in
the Hall who had not caught a glimpse of the bundle of
letters he had carried under his arm as he entered.

'I am aware that the matter of the attacks mentioned here
on Monday has excited some interest,' he said amid complete
silence. 'This may well be a sensation, which is ill-founded,
but I have received a number of communications relative to
the individual who is said to be occupied in winning a wager
by appearing in various terrific characters at night in the
villages round the metropolis. The Recorder will now read a
selection of these.'

With that Sir John handed down his bundle to the Recorder. For a moment the man was almost taken aback by
the thickness of the pile; then holding up the first missive he
began to read:

My Lord Mayor — The Public are much indebted to your Lordship
for bringing forward the letter, as stated in yesterday's Mansion
House report. Although there is yet no authenticity given to that

part of the letter in which it is stated lámentable accidents have arisen from this wicked prank, that it has been played off lately to a considerable extent in the neighbouring villages I can assure your Lordship to be a fact.

In the neighbourhood of Hornsey, where I have a residence, some scoundrel has been alarming the neighbourhood in these disguises, and I heard yesterday in our news-room at Guildhall, from one of the deputies, that the same thing has been played off near Kingston, and from a respectable neighbour in Cheapside that Hertfordshire has been similarly visited.

It is stated that some individual ('gentleman' he has been designated) drives about with a livery servant in a cab, and, throwing off a cloak, appears in these frightful forms, and is to win a wager by the joke — if it be a joke, one that is very likely to produce the catastrophe detailed in the letter but which, till the writer comes forward and acknowledges it, cannot be considered as fact.

I should rather incline to think it is some determined thief who visits houses in the absence of the heads of families, and who seeks by this method of at once paralysing the energies of the servants to obtain and escape with his booty on easy terms.

I shall shortly remove my family from my town residence to that above stated, where if I catch Mr Ghost on any part of my premises, I shall administer that to this substantial part that if ever he reappears it shall be only his serial essence, or as a ghost in fact.

Other heads of families in my neighbourhood having expressed the same determination, I trust the ghost will soon be laid; mean time publicity to the matter will do good, and attract the notice of the authorities without the city.

The Recorder paused briefly to look at the top and bottom of the letter before giving the writer's name and address as Thomas Lott of Bow Lane, London. There was no outburst of chatter as he finished — there was such food for thought in all the implications of the letter, that no one had time to voice any opinion to his neighbour before the Recorder took up a second letter. This was to prove from a still more important and creditable source — a magistrate of Peckham where the first report had originated:

I am induced to address your Lordship on the subject of the Peckham ghost to which I perceive, by this morning's paper, your attention has been called. I will promise that I am an acting magistrate for this county, and a practising barrister. I mention this as a guarantee that I will not improperly trespass upon your Lordship's valuable time.

Some few weeks ago an old female domestic, who lived in my service many years, and who now resides in respectable circumstances, as the wife of a decent tradesman at Hammersmith, called upon me, and in the course of conversation informed me that the females of Hammersmith and its vicinity feared to walk abroad after nightfall in consequence of the molestations of a ghost or monster to which they were exposed.

At first I, with your Lordship, thought this visitation in the 19th Century, so near the metropolis, and with such a well organised police as we now have, too absurd for belief; but on further inquiry I ascertained that several young women had really been frighted into fits — dangerous fits and some of them had been severely wounded by a sort of claws the miscreant wore on his hands.

I expressed my surprise that the attention of the police had not been called to the nuisance. My informant assured me that repeatedly their vigilance had been aroused on the subject, but the fellow or fellows had been adroit enough to elude capture. I have that reliance on the witness I allude to, that I have no doubt she reported facts.

On perusing your Lordship's observations this morning, which were precisely of the same kind as my own when I first heard of the matter, I deemed it my duty to communicate the above facts to your Lordship.

I will take an opportunity of more minutely inquiring into this affair should the investigation which the police will no doubt institute fáil of fully detecting the miscreants who are undoubtedly working real mischief, though under a childish and grotesque disguise.

Now a hub-bub of conversation sprang up all over the Common Hall. Those who had believed in the story all along, turned triumphantly on companions who had doubted. Could anyone dismiss the matter now after such expert evidence? And what further puzzles the letter had thrown up! How indeed could such a person outwit the police? And might there possibly be more than one such villain?

There were even more surprises in store as the next letter was read out:

Your Lordship will, I trust, pardon the liberty I have been induced to take in addressing your Lordship. My reason for so doing is to inform you that the letter you received a few days ago respecting some person who makes it his delight to frighten the peaceable inhabitants of the suburbs of the metropolis is not without foundation.

He has frightened several persons in Stockwell, Brixton, Camberwell and Vauxhall, and has caused the death of several; and many instances can be proved of his frightening people into fits.

Hoping you will not think lightly of this matter, I am your Lordship's faithful and obedient servant — An Inhabitant of Stockwell.

The Recorder's last words were drowned in gasps of astonishment, and one of the newspaper reporters was to note later that, 'there was a lady who fainted right away at this extraordinary revelation, and not a few others cried out in fear at such news'. Strong men paled, too, and the Recorder glanced up at Sir John to see if he should continue.

Raising his hand for silence, the Lord Mayor said that there were many other letters of a similar nature which he did not propose to have read out at this moment. However there were two more which he felt should be published, the first which had been addressed to Mr Hobler, the city solicitor, whom he would ask to read it out.

The solicitor rose from his bench, and taking a scrap of paper from the Recorder, read what had been written to him:

There have been rumours in St. John's Wood and its neighbourhood, for the last fortnight, of the appearance of the monster alluded to in the police report of yesterday of the Mansion House, inserted in *The Times* this morning.

The bet is, however, understood to be of an even more grave nature than is there stated, and, if it be true, amounts to murder. As far as the writer had been informed, the bet is, that the monster shall kill six women in some given time.

It is asserted that he has been seen in St. John's Wood clad in mail, and as a bear.

Again cries of surprise and alarm rang around the hall. Each letter seemed to pile horror upon horror. Could there be still more to come in the other letter the Lord Mayor had mentioned?

As soon as Mr Hobler had sat down the Recorder picked up the final letter which he said had been sent to Sir John by a man who lived in Lewisham and signed himself 'J.C.'. It ran:

> On reading the letter in the papers of this day received by your Lordship, I perceive that you are not inclined to give credence to the account furnished by your correspondent.
>
> The villain mentioned in it as appearing in the guise of a ghost, bear and devil, has been within the last week or two repeatedly seen in Lewisham and Blackheath. So much, indeed, has he frightened the inhabitants of those peaceful districts, that women and children durst not stir out of their houses after dark.
>
> There ought to be a stop put to this; but the police, I am afraid, are frightened at him also. . . .

There was silence from the packed hall this time, and looks of bewilderment replaced those of surprise. If even the police were frightened of this devil, London was surely in for a time of terror And supposing that he now moved his activities into the very heart of the city?

After the Recorder had carefully gathered up the sheaths of paper and returned them to Sir John, the Lord Mayor looked up and began to speak. By the tone of his voice it was clear he felt some element of calm needed to be restored.

'It is evident,' he said, 'that considerable terror has been excited by the appearance of some man or men in the outlets of the metropolis in disguise, and that a great deal of mischief might arise from a pantomimic display at night in a retired and peaceful neighbourhood.

'*But--*', and he laid considerable emphasis on the word, 'I have thought from the first that the greatest exaggerations have been made. I believe it to be quite impossible that there could be any foundation in the report that the ghost performs the feats of a devil upon earth. I must also withold my credence from the statement that so many ladies have been frightened to death. Nonetheless,' (and again his tone changed slightly) 'I have been given to understand from an authority which I cannot question, that one of the female servants of a gentleman who resides near my house at Forest Hill, beyond Peckham, was a short time since terrified into fits by the sudden appearance of a figure clad in a bear's skin.'

So Sir John was having second thoughts. He may not believe all the stories, but could not deny there was more than a little truth in the accounts.

Mr Hobbler, the city solicitor, was, however, less convinced of the serious nature of the business, as he indicated when he rose to give a short address.

'I believe that in all probability the matter will end one day in a good ducking. If anything serious has resulted from the tricks which are said to have already been played, the police will no doubt have been apprised of it.

'That some mischievous fellows, who deserve to be well trounced are at work, though, there exists no doubt,' he added.

In his closing remarks, the Lord Mayor sought to indicate that while the evidence did point to some unpleasant activities taking place in the area, there was no reason why the matter should not be speedily cleared up. A smile broke out on his face, as if he wished to ease still further the tension in the room. 'I trust,' he went on, 'that the fears which are being entertained by you will soon vanish altogether. I have the satisfaction of knowing that I have the assistance of a barrister and an attorney whose names and respectability are above reproach, and all I can say is that if two lawyers cannot make a fool of the devil himself between them, then I do not know who the d----l can!'

As the court reporters noted, there was laughter around the official benches at this closing remark. But it was not repeated among the listening crowd.

Indeed it was a much more sombre audience that filed out of the Mansion House that day to pass on the news to those still waiting outside. Whatever the Lord Mayor and his assistants had said, there had been much in those letters to confirm the people's fears about the demon attacker of London. If he was not caught soon, who knew where or against whom he might strike next?

And it was as the crowds began to disperse across the city

33

still earnestly discussing what they had heard, that someone made the observation that this mysterious creature seemed able to escape from his crimes with great speed. 'He's a real spring-ald' the same voice said.

Unconsciously, a legend had been born.

3

The Reign of Terror

Although it was the disclosures by the Lord Mayor in January 1838 which first brought the activities of Spring Heeled Jack to national attention, the leaping demon had in fact been on the prowl since the previous Autumn.

The publicity which was generated as a result of the correspondence Sir John Cowan received could, in hindsight, almost be said to have breached the 'censorship' of the story — if censorship there was. Certainly a most exhaustive checking of the press in the months prior to the Mansion House meetings fails to produce a single mention of an agile criminal at work in the environs of London. Although it would be difficult to substantiate a claim that the press deliberately made no mention of the attacks, it is strange to find that a story which was so obviously a topic of local gossip in several areas of the metropolis did not reach the ears of at least one alert reporter or sensation-seeking editor.

But silence there had indeed been, until Sir John's attempt to play down — even be slightly scornful of — the claims of the 'Resident of Peckham' had brought such an astonishing and voluminous post in reply.

However, if we move back in time to late September 1837 we can trace the first authenticated report of the man who was to become notorious as Spring Heeled Jack.

The setting for his first appearance could hardly have been more appropriate — or more guaranteed to give rise to the most chilling rumours. The site was close by the old cemetery standing on Barnes Common in Middlesex.

Barnes Common, on the Southern Bank of the River Thames just where it makes one of its most picturesque sweeping bends, was in 1837 a rather isolated spot on the outskirts of London. It had for years enjoyed a rather unsavoury reputation, and those foolhardy enough to walk across it in poor weather or at night ran the very real danger of being attacked and robbed. Assaults were commonplace, and few people who lived in the vicinity were not familiar with the story of the butcher who had been murdered there and left in a huge pool of blood. For years after this, it was said no grass would grow on the spot where the body had lain.

Even the district immediately bordering on the Common was shunned, particularly the area around one large turreted house where a particularly atrocious double-murder had taken place. It was said, too, that the Common was a favourite spot for suicides.

As if all this was not enough, there were stories of a ghost which haunted the misty blackness of the cemetery, and in the past the graveyard had more than once been subjected to the attentions of body snatchers.

It was here during the space of two evenings in late September that a man hurrying home from his business and three inoffensive working girls were confronted by the leaping terror.

The man had been detained late at his office in Barnes and was taking a short cut across the Common to his home in Putney. He said later he had scarcely taken any notice of his surroundings as he hurried by the cemetery, so engrossed was he in thoughts of business. Then suddenly, from over the railings which surrounded the graveyard, had appeared what seemed like 'the very devil himself'. He had instantly taken to his heels without waiting to see more.

The following night it was the turn of three different girls, also homeward bound in the gathering gloom, to come face to face with the horror. Each had walked along the southern side of the cemetery and was pounced upon by the figure who cleared the railings at a bound.

The first girl was seized and had her coat torn by the assailant before she managed to struggle free. The second was knocked to the ground but not touched by the 'vision' who merely grinned at her 'with eyes of flame' as she regained her feet and fled back the way she had come. The third girl was actually pulled over, her clothes torn from her body, and she was left nearly naked and unconscious on the ground, where a patrolling policeman eventually found her. All three later said the thing they most clearly remembered was the weird, ringing laughter that issued from their assailant.

Although, as I have said, these attacks were not reported in a single newspaper, the details of them were very quickly in the province of local gossip. And in the weeks that followed, the mystery assailant was to strike again and again in Middlesex, primarily in small copses and the remoter lanes.

For several days in early October he concentrated his activities on the area of Clapham Common, beginning in the singularly appropriate location of Cut-Throat Lane.

At this time the Common was a huge expanse of gorse-covered land surrounded by sizeable detached houses owned in the main by London merchants, all of which had high walled gardens and shuttered windows. It was a place which attracted burglars and footpads galore and was not somewhere to be out on at night.

Cut-Throat Lane no longer exists today, but in 1837 there was a narrow, rather winding passage leading from Clapham Common to Lavender Hill. It was regarded with suspicion and superstition by local people and there were tales of lonely travellers being robbed there and faithless sweethearts lured to the spot by jealous lovers to have their throats cut. Truly, it deserved its name!

It was here that a certain Mary Stevens was hurrying back one evening to the big house on Lavender Hill where she was employed as a servant. She had been to visit her family at their home on the Battersea marshes and as she reached the turnstile at the entrance to Cut-Throat Lane she felt rain begin to patter on her face.

Then suddenly out of the darkness a tall, black figure leapt over the stile with a single bound and clasped her in his arms. She felt a man's lips on her face, a hand plunging into her bosom, and a loud laugh split the silence.

Almost immediately afterwards a scream broke from Mary's lips and at that her attacker turned and vanished into the night. Her cries soon brought a group of men from the nearby 'Falcon Hotel' and they organised a search for the mystery man — but to no avail.

At first the concensus of opinion was that Mary, who was something of a highly-strung girl, and nervous of the dark, had imagined the incident. But the next night another event occurred which confirmed that the agile terror was in the neighbourhood.

A carriage returning from London was almost wrecked by the horses running away in Streatham High Road, which was quite close to Lavender Hill, though on the other side of the common. Both the coachman and footman were badly injured in the ensuing crash, and said that the accident had occurred when a huge creature, "whether man or bird or beast they could not say" had leapt from the shadows on one side of the way and sprung clean across the wide road, vanishing over a high wall.

Even the sceptics were dumbfounded at this, and then as final proof a lady walking home in the dusk after visiting friends in Clapham village was confronted. The woman was accompanied by her two young sons, and half-way home realised she had left some sewing behind. She dispatched the boys back to collect it while she sat down to wait for them beside the railings of Clapham Churchyard.

As the boys hurried back the way they had come, they met a solitary pedestrian whom they later described as being a tall young man, very slimly built and wearing dark clothes with a cape coat. His hat was pulled down over his eyes so that they could not see his face.

A short while after they had passed him, the boys heard screams and recognised the voice of their mother. Immediately they turned and ran back to find her clinging terrified to the railings.

When she had sufficiently regained her composure she said she had been accosted by a black figure who had then bounded away into the church-yard.

By this time, tales of the mysterious assailant in the area of the Common were well-known, and after the alarm was raised by the two boys, a thorough search was quickly made of the surrounding area.

No sign of the man was found, however — though two deep footprints were spotted just on the other side of the church-yard wall. They had all the appearance of having been made by someone who had landed from a height.

More intriguing still was the curious shape of the prints which eye-witnesses later said gave the impression that the man must have had "machines" or springs attached to his shoes. Unfortunately, before anyone with expert knowledge could examine the marks, they were allowed to become obliterated.

It was the first real clue to the secret of his agility that the mystery man had left.

Soon he was apparently spreading his circle of operations on a wider scale still, and there were reports with every indication of authenticity from East Sheen, Richmond, Ham, Kingston and Hampton. By the middle of October he was visiting lonely spots at Teddington, Twickenham, Hounslow and Uxbridge as well.

Naturally rumour had gathered together the various accounts, and there was no denying a striking similarity about all the descriptions of the unearthly bogeyman. This seemed to put paid to the first idea that the attacks were the handiwork of a gang of maniacs got up in bizarre costumes. It seemed that they had all been perpetrated by a single criminal of almost supernatural capabilities.

The picture which emerged of the attacker was this. He was tall, enormously powerful and very agile. He wore a long, flowing cloak and black, high-heeled boots. Of his face it was said he had fiery eyes, a prominent nose, and ears which appeared to be pointed. Every victim had also felt the iron grip of his fingers which, they said, resembled claws.

Throughout the rest of the month, and on into November and December, Spring Heeled Jack (if I may be allowed to use the term, though this was not yet how people were describing him) continued to plague the London environs, growing bolder and more outrageous with the passage of time. He travelled still further afield. In Dulwich he cornered two young

girls in a lane and, with one swooning in his right arm, proceeded to pull the dress off the other with his free hand. In
Forest Hill he surprised a gentleman and his lady strolling
home from dining out, slashed the man across the face with
his claws and half-blinded the woman 'with the foul fumes
which emitted from his lips'. And in Camberwell he attacked
the young daughter of a local dignitary while it was still
almost light. Once again his laughter followed his escape and
remained ringing in the minds of these people for many days
afterwards.

Only once were his intentions seemingly frustrated. A
benevolent lady who was in the habit of taking food to a
gypsy encampment on Tooting Bec Common was returning
from one of her missions when she suddenly saw a figure
bounding towards her out of the evening mist. She sensed
immediately who it must be and let out a piercing scream.

Fortunately, she was still within earshot of the encampment, and a group of the gypsy men raced to her rescue. The
men were in fact so quickly on the scene that the mystery
man had barely reached his prospective victim and, seeing
them arrive, was forced to turn and speed away.

Even though he was soon lost in the mist, the woman saw
him quite clearly and was firmly convinced that he was a
flesh and blood mortal.

Indeed, her account given later is one of the very few to
indicate that Jack was not without his limitations and needed
all the help he could get to successfully carry out his attacks.
"He was doing far more than an ordinary man could have
accomplished without mechanical aid," the lady said, "but
nothing resembling the exploits which he was credited by
rumour. Had a good horse been near he could have been over-
taken, but as it was he escaped, the mist and gathering night
helping him."

The pattern of the attacks was unvaryingly similar. The
phantom leapt upon his victims with huge bounds, tearing
their clothes and scaring them half to death. Yet what was his
purpose, people began to ask? Young, pretty girls seemed his
favourite targets, yet although he stripped them virtually
naked, not one was raped or even interfered with. Was he
some kind of weird voyeur — or did he nurture a grievance

40

against the female of the species which made him want to degrade them in some way? It was certainly a puzzle — and it seemed hard to credit the idea that it might just be a series of pranks.

Such was the growing atmosphere of tension as the year drew to its close. The weather turned bitter, people felt less inclined to go out except when it was essential, and consequently the number of attacks grew fewer. But the feeling of unease was mounting steadily. In Middlesex particularly people began to ask: Is nobody going to say anything about this menace? And, more importantly, is nobody going to do anything?

The answer, of course, came with the revelations early in the New Year at the Mansion House. The tremendous public response to the publication of details about the leaping terror of London had a number of significant effects on the authorities.

Sir John Cowan, the Lord Mayor, for one, admitted that his initial scepticism had undergone a change, and when he met in assembly on the curiously appropriate following Friday, the thirteenth of January, announced that he had approved the setting up of a vigilante committee to try and track the man down. This body was to consist of magistrates, army officers and ordinary citizens. Sir John stressed that there must be no taking the law into their own hands, and that the vigilantes, each and every one, were charged with bringing the man into custody if they should catch him. He himself regretted that he could now 'do no more in the matter' and hoped that these other authorities would be successful in the hunt.

This announcement at first surprised people, but to be fair, it has to be pointed out that Sir John did not withdraw his interest in the matter lightly, or because he still harboured doubts about the reports. His hands were full with other matters for on the Wednesday night the Royal Exchange had been burnt down in a terrible fire with, consequently, much disruption to London life which required his attention rather more than the elusive bogeyman. Also, the villain was still

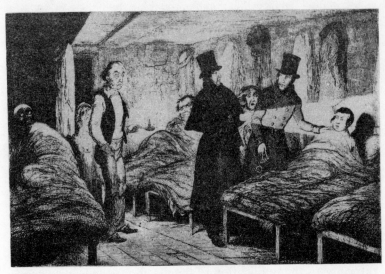

'Peelers' searching a London lodging house. An engraving by George Cruikshank.

only operating outside the city limits.

The police, too, were soon actively deployed in the hunt, and horse patrols were organised to scour the suburban districts. Foot patrols in the locations where the attacks had taken place were doubled, and many of the earlier victims were seen again by detective police officers in the hope that they might provide some fresh clues.

To the more cynical of the population, this should have all begun much sooner, but as if to underline just how seriously the whole matter was now being treated, two of the nation's most distinguished men-of-war leant their more than considerable weight to the hunt. They were the Battle of Trafalgar veteran, Admiral Codrington, and the vanquisher of Napoleon, the grand old Duke of Wellington.

Admiral Sir Edward Codrington (1770-1851) entered the Navy as a teenager and had a meteoric rise through the ranks, high-lighting his career at sea in October 1805 when he commanded a squadron at the Battle of Trafalgar. In 1826 he became Commander-in-Chief of the Mediterranean fleet and played a leading role in the destruction of the Turkish fleet at Navarino (for which he was awarded the G.C.B.). Following this he became land based, being made an Admiral in 1837, and devoting himself to a number of social causes. Living in London, he was a keen disciplinarian and strong upholder of law and order, and it was this which gave him a particular feeling of outrage when he read of the activities of the district's agile assailant.

Following the two meetings at the Mansion House, Admiral Codrington wrote to the Lord Mayor offering to personally organise a reward fund for the apprehension of the criminal. 'The posting of such a reward,' he wrote, 'will surely encourage the proffering of any information which will lead to the seizure of this brutal molester of innocent females. I shall be pleased to open this fund with a donation of £100.'

Admiral Codrington — organiser of the fund to catch the 'Terror of London'.

Admiral Codrington's idea was enthusiastically received at the Mansion House and a number of other London notables subsequently contributed to it until its value exceeded £1,000. Yet it was all to no avail — and to the best of my knowledge that reward lies unclaimed in a London bank to this day.

The lure of money to perhaps tempt an informer was one way of tackling the problem, but to a military man like the Duke of Wellington something far more practical was what was really required. He had always believed in direct action — and that was just what he favoured in this instance.

Arthur Wellesley, 1st Duke of Wellington (1769-1852), lead a somewhat dilettante life as a young man, but taking up soldiering distinguished himself by his bravery and as a military administrator. There followed successful campaigns in Egypt and India, where he was created a K.B. for his services, and then as a result of the emergence of Napoleon it quickly became apparent that he was one of the few British soldiers knowledgeable and tactically-skilled enough to take on and defeat the upstart Corsican. Wellington's subsequent victory with his inferior army at Waterloo is one of the great moments of British military history. The Duke's interest in crime and criminals had been particularly stimulated when in 1829 he helped Sir Robert Peel in his organisation of the Metropolitan Police.

However, so incensed was he by the reports in January 1838 of this leaping marauder that he vowed to track the man down himself. Despite his advancing years — he was nearly 70 — the Duke set out each night on horseback from his London home to patrol Spring Heeled Jack's likely locations. Even he, though, was not prepared to underestimate his opponent, and, to his saddle bow, he attached holsters in which he carried his most trusty pistols.

The sight of this marvellous and much revered old man setting off in the dusk each evening was said to have been watched by many London citizens and, according to one report, 'so cheered those who saw him that they felt able to sleep easy in their beds that night.'

It was a spirited gesture — but also destined to come to nothing. For even the man who had taken on and defeated

The Duke of Wellington, who set out on horseback to capture Spring Heeled Jack.

some of the world's most feared armies and their commanders, could not deter the leaping terror of southern London.

With the passing of the weeks, the lanes and commons around London increasingly became places of dread. The population rapidly found themselves in the grip of a considerable panic. Only the foolhardy would venture there by night, and families who by day had once walked carefree across such open spaces avoided them as if the plague were abroad. Indeed the mysterious attacker was now regarded as having almost supernatural powers — certainly no one seemed to have the faintest idea how to catch him or even stop him — and his ability and the ferocity of his attacks were beyond question. Fear of him mounted day by day.

A contemporary report notes, 'Starting south of the river (the man) had worked upstream to the westwards before crossing the Thames at Teddington. Then he worked his way from village to village until he reached the grounds of Kensington Palace, where he stayed some time. He was seen climbing over the park wall at midnight and dancing fantastic measures on the wooded lawns. His itinerary had taken him on a circuit of the metropolis, avoiding towns, and leaving a trail of unnerved villagers behind him. *It was odd that he seemed to base himself on private parks, resting a few days in each.*'

I shall be returning to the significance of the words I have italicised later in the book.

In any event, confusion seemed to beset everyone, private citizen and official alike — typified by some of the unfortunate stories about the activities of the Lord Mayor's vigilantes. On several occasions men in these bands had set upon innocent citizens who they had mistakenly thought to be the assailant. The top-hatted police had suffered most in this way — the shadows they threw in dingy streets could be contorted into the most unearthly shapes and to nervous minds quickly took on the appearance of the hunted criminal. As a result of this a number of policemen were quite badly beaten before they could gasp out their real identities.

The newspapers were in a state verging on hysteria. They were unable to recall any other criminal who had so easily defied the laws — both the laws of man and of nature. For while he outraged the public safety, did he not also defy physical laws with the agility of his attack?

It was in late January 1838, that the references to the attacker suddenly changed from the vague 'Leaping Terror' and 'Suburban Ghost' — to name but two — to the more specific 'Springald' — a jumping jack. For there was now a growing conviction among those who dismissed the idea that he possessed super-natural powers, that he had some kind of springs concealed in his boots which enabled him to carry out his enormous leaps.

From 'Springald' it was only a twist of the tongue and a journalist's pen to the full-blown 'Spring Heeled Jack'; which became the mystery man's appellation for once and all.

And — perhaps because his reputation was now secure — Jack at last felt the time was right to move into the confines of London itself. He also prepared for his most audacious confrontation to date.

Lucy and Margaret Scales were two pretty teenage sisters who lived in the Limehouse district of London. Though today Limehouse is regarded as one of the tougher areas of the capital, in February 1838 it was predominantly a respectable neighbourhood with some fine houses and shops owned by hard-working and mainly comfortably-off citizens. It was a place where two girls might reasonably expect to be able to walk home after an evening visit to a relative without undue danger. But that was until the night of Wednesday February 18.

On this evening, 18-year-old Lucy, and Margaret, who was a year younger, had spent a pleasant evening with their elder brother, Tom, at his home in Narrow Street, Limehouse. Tom lived above the butcher's shop which was his business and was a well-respected local figure. The girls had passed the time playing cards and drinking tea before leaving to walk the short distance home. They had left at 8.35 so as to be home by quarter to nine as instructed by their father.

After fond goodbyes, Lucy had walked purposefully up the street with Margaret skipping behind playing hopscotch. At the corner of Narrow Street, she was just about to turn into Green Dragon Alley when she hesitated. This dimly lit passageway which ran beside a public house, provided the Scales's sisters with an ideal short cut home. But as Lucy passed it while waiting for Margaret to catch up, she suddenly noticed something out of the corner of her eye.

A shadow moved just inside the passageway. Lucy brushed

some strands of her long blonde hair out of her eyes and took a few steps forward. There seemed to be a figure lurking at an angle in the alley. Lucy stopped for an instant and heard the sing-song voice of her sister as she drew nearer behind, still intent on her game; but at that moment the figure in the shadows pounced on her.

It all happened in an instant, but Lucy saw a tall, thin man, enveloped in a long black cloak. In front of him he was carrying what looked like a bulls-eye lantern. With one bound he was in front of her, and before she had a chance to move, he had belched blue flames from this mouth into her face.

With a scream of terror as the hot fire momentarily blinded her, Lucy fell back onto the ground. Her screams rang out into the night air as she rolled about in agony, hands pressed to her eyes. At this her assailant merely turned calmly round and faded quickly into the shadows.

Hearing her sister's cries, Margaret rushed into the passageway and found Lucy lying on the floor. She immediately burst into tears.

Fortunately for the girls, brother Tom had been standing on his doorway watching them safely down the street, and he heard the cries and saw Margaret running panic-stricken into Green Dragon Alley. He raced quickly after her and was at the side of his sister Lucy only moments later. He could tell at a glance she had been attacked, but there was no sign of anyone nearby when he looked up.

Gently lifting Lucy into his arms, Tom carried her carefully back to his house. By now people were appearing from everywhere after hearing the cries. The hysterical sobbing of the girl clearly indicated she had been molested. But by whom?

It was the following morning before Lucy had recovered enough from her shock and terror to describe her assailant. And there could be no doubting from her picture that the man had been Spring Heeled Jack.

The news spread across Limehouse and through the environs of the city with electrifying speed. The monster was now loose in the city itself.

The 'tall, thin, gentlemanly' criminal was obviously growing bolder, and two days later instigated his most audacious

48

attack yet. The setting was the home of Mr James Alsop, a gentleman of considerable property, of Bearbind Cottage, in Bearbind Lane, at Bow in East London.

Mr Alsop, an elderly and rather frail man, had been ill for some weeks, and was confined to bed with a rheumatic affliction. His wife was also in poor health, and on the evening in question the two old people were in their bedroom being entertained by their three daughters, Mary, 16, Jane, 18, and a married daughter, Mrs Sarah Harrison, who had called in for a few hours. The old folk were propped up in their beds with pillows, while their daughters sat around the cosy fireplace, talking and telling stories.

Suddenly this cheerful domestic scene was shattered by the violent ringing of the bell at the front gate.

A frown creased Mr Alsop's brow. He took up his watch from his bedside table and opened the front. It was just after a quarter to nine. Who on earth could be calling at this hour of the night?

As the bell continued to jangle, Jane Alsop, Mr Alsop's 18-year-old daughter stood up, and asked her father if he would like her to go downstairs and see who it was? He smiled across at the pretty brunette and nodded.

Putting down her book, Jane walked out of the room, down the stairs, along the hallway and opened the front door. At first she could see nothing in the gloom. Then out in the shadows she saw a figure who seemed to be wearing a top-hat and cloak.

For a moment there was silence as Jane waited for the figure to speak. Then holding up one hand she said, 'Please do not ring so loud. What is the matter?' She was reluctant to leave the doorstep as it was a cold, dark night outside.

Immediately the figure replied, 'I am a policeman.' He seemed to take a huge step forward and Jane thought his appearance seemed like that of a member of the horse patrol.

Another step and the voice went on hoarsely, 'For God's sake bring me a light, for we have caught Spring Heeled Jack here in the lane!'

Jane's heart missed a beat and she shivered involuntarily. She had of course heard all about the agile criminal — and that he was now supposed to be on the loose in London. Had they at last caught him? That would be good news!

Without a second thought she hurried back into the house and fetched a lighted candle which stood in the hallway. The instant she returned and held it out to the man, she knew she had made a mistake — a terrible mistake.

For the figure threw down his cloak onto the ground to reveal the hideous features of Spring Heeled Jack himself!

The following morning the young girl was to repeat what happened in the next few nightmare minutes to the local Magistrate, Mr Hardwick, at Lambeth Street Police Office. Her statement remains to this day a vivid picture and perhaps even more evocative than any retelling of the outrage could hope to be:

> She returned into the house and brought a candle and handed it to the person, who appeared enveloped in a large cloak, and whom she at first really believed to be a policeman. The instant she had done so, however, he threw off his outer garment, and applying the lighted candle to his breast, presented a most hideous and frightful appearance, and vomitted forth a quantity of blue and white flame from his mouth, and his eyes resembled red balls of fire.
>
> From the hasty glance which her fright enabled her to get at his person, she observed that he wore a large helmet; and his dress, which appeared to fit him very tight, seemed to her to resemble white oilskin. Without uttering a sentence he darted at her, and catching her partly by the dress and the back part of her neck, placed her head under one of his arms, and commenced tearing her gown with his claws, which she was certain were of some metallic substance.
>
> She screamed out as loud as she could for assistance, and by considerable exertion got away from him and ran towards the house to get in. Her assailant, however, followed her, and caught her on the steps leading to the hall-door, where he again used considerable violence, tore her neck and arms with his claws, as well as a quantity of hair from her head; but she was at length rescued from his grasp by one of her sisters.
>
> Miss Alsop added that she suffered considerably all night from the shock she had sustained, and was then in extreme pain, both from injury done to her arm, and the wounds and scratches inflicted by the miscreant about her shoulders and neck with his claws or hands.

The other members of the Alsop household also gave accounts of their parts in the drama, beginning with Mary Alsop, Jane's younger sister, who was first on the scene. Her statement reads:

> Miss Mary Alsop, a younger sister, said that on hearing the screams of her sister Jane, she went to the door, and saw a figure as already described, ill-using her sister. She was so alarmed at his appearance, that she was afraid to approach or render any assistance.

The third, and eldest, sister, Mrs Harrison, arrived next and proved herself resourceful and brave — taking the fight to Spring Heeled Jack: the first woman to have done so. Her statement to Mr Hardwick ran thus:

> Mrs Harrison said that hearing the screams of both her sisters, first Jane and then of Mary, she ran downstairs to the door, and found the person before described in the act of dragging her sister Jane down the steps from the door with considerable violence. She (Mrs Harrison) got hold of her sister, and by some means or other, which she could scarcely describe, succeeded in getting her inside the door and closing it.
>
> At this time her sister's dress was nearly torn off her, both her combs dragged out of her head, as well as a quantity of her hair torn away.
>
> The fellow, notwithstanding the outrage he had committed, knocked loudly two or three times at the door, and it was only on their calling loudly for the police from the upper windows that he left the place.

Poor old Mr Alsop, who had heard the screaming of his daughters, did the best he could to raise himself from his bed. Despite his infirmity, concern for his off-spring gave him unexpected strength and he managed to struggle downstairs. His alarm was fully justified, he later told the Magistrate, when he found Susan with her clothes torn and all the appearance of having received the most serious personal violence.

Mr Alsop is also recorded as having told Mr Hardwick that he believed it was 'perfectly clear' that there was more than one ruffian connected with the outrage 'as the fellow who committed the violence did not return for his cloak, but scampered across the fields, *so that there must have been some person with him to pick it up.*'

Such was the audacious attack carried out on the Alsop family. Perhaps flushed with his success and daring, Spring Heeled Jack tried the same trick again on the following Friday, February 27, when he appeared at the doorway of a house belonging to a Mr Ashworth in Turner Street, off Commercial Road. This time, though, he was answered by a servant boy.

Muffled behind his black cloak, the figure asked in a gruff voice to speak with the boy's master. As the youngster turned to leave, the visitor moved half out of the shadows, and he caught sight of a pair of fiery, staring eyes and the glint of light on a claw-like hand.

Fiery eyes? A claw-like hand? The boy knew all about the stories of Spring Heeled Jack. His panic released his vocal chords and he began to scream the place down.

As doors and windows nearby began to clatter open, Jack turned from the doorway and with several enormous bounds was down the street and lost in the darkness. This was the second time that a mission was unsuccessful. But it was the first time he had presented what looked like a real clue to his identity. For under cross-examination the following day, the servant boy swore that on the folds of the man's cloak, just above the corner which he clutched to his face with his claw-like hand, he had seen *an ornate crest of some kind — and below it, in gold filigree, the initial 'W'.*

4

Who was Spring Heeled Jack?

Despite his notoriety at the time of his reign of terror in London during 1837-8, Spring Heeled Jack has received little attention since then from historians and criminologists. With the passing of the years he has become little more than a footnote in criminal history, although his name has, as I have already mentioned, become part of our language. There has not been any serious attempt to reveal Jack's identity as has been the case with the Ripper, and, perhaps because no one has been prepared to investigate the facts, his criminal persona has been glossed over in the vaguest terms. 'A lunatic pieman who committed suicide in the River Thames before he was caught' has been one suggestion. Or 'an escaped inmate of an asylum whose deformed features gave rise to the descriptions of fiery eyes & etc.,' to quote another.

Historian Elizabeth Villiers has reported that not so long ago a writer suggested that Jack might not have been a human being at all — but a kangaroo! This author speculated that the animal had escaped from captivity and found hiding places in the wooded gardens on the outskirts of London. Then after being recaptured, its owner hushed the story up lest he should get into trouble with the authorities for keeping such a pet.

Miss Villiers admits that at the time Australia was an almost unknown land, and though accounts of the kangaroo had reached England, many quite educated people declined to believe such animals existed. "That being the case," she argues "if one had been brought to London it would have been impossible to keep its presence a secret, and in the face of that the belated explanation may be dismissed."

I think it is high time we tried to establish precisely who this cunning, ingenious, but certainly reprehensible rogue might have been. And the answer is as surprising as it is simple.

For it is my conviction that the man who invented the character of Spring Heeled Jack and performed the bizarre exploits which we have recorded in the years 1837-8 was a eccentric young Irish nobleman, Henry, Marquis of Waterford.

This assertion is based on exhaustive study of the available records and a detailed investigation into the Marquis's whereabouts at the times of the Spring Heeled Jack crimes, but perhaps more important still; on the clues presented to us by the leaping terror himself.

I say that I find the solution as simple as it is surprising because the Marquis was undisputed as one of the most notorious practical jokers and perpetrators of wild stunts of the period; a man given to undertaking any crazy scheme for the sake of the experience and totally incapable of resisting any wager. 'Challenge Waterford to a bet,' it was said, 'and he's your man whatever the odds.'

As we shall see, the exploits of Spring Heeled Jack were wholly within his capabilities — and the facts seal the case, though of course there is no way now that he can be summoned to answer the charges beyond all reasonable doubt.

Before examining the clues that Jack himself left as to his identity, let us study the recorded evidence about the wild life of the nobleman who came from Waterford, on the picturesque southern coast of Ireland.

Henry de la Poer Beresford, Marquis of Waterford and also Baron Tyrone of Haverfordwest, was born on April 26, 1811, into one of the richest and most privileged families in Ireland. His father, Lord John Beresford, was a renowned figure in both Britain and Ireland, a great landowner and social benefactor.

Henry was a dark, curly-haired, sturdy child whose other-

54

wise handsome features were slightly marred by protruding eyes. Only once did a child make fun of these 'pop eyes' and received such a beating that afterwards no one dared risk voicing another affront. In fact, from quite an early age, Henry showed himself to be strong, resourceful, exceptionally quick-witted and with a sense of mischief that rapidly developed into an obsession.

At Eton, which he attended from 1824 to 1926, his practical jokes were ceaseless and his skill at fisticuffs legendary. His sporting qualities indeed put him head and shoulders over most of his contemporaries and it is recorded that he was the best oarsman in the College Eight of 1829. When he

The Marquis of Waterford in 1837 — Spring Heeled Jack.

moved on to Oxford and found himself in the same company with other young noblemen and bucks to whom money was no object and the search for excitement and stimulation unending, he quickly flowered into a hell-raiser and heavy gambler. After his matriculation from Oxford in October 1829 he moved straight to London. He was just 18 years old and thirsty for pleasure.

The early years of the nineteenth century have been called a 'golden age' for the 'man of pleasure' when those of good breeding with wealthy and indulgent parents, could get up to highly unconventional and even brutal escapades and were shown the most amazing toleration. The worst spot of trouble which might befall these bloods, was a night in the cells of Vine Street and a fine the following morning at Marlborough Street Police Office. They were a recognisable type, in fact, who devoted themselves to 'sport' in a London where Regent Street had only just been constructed (in 1813) and the suburbs were all rural in character (Chelsea, for instance, was still approachable across green fields!).

The young bucks like Waterford were attracted to the sporting hotels which gave anyone fresh up from a country a swift education into the ways of the capital. In his admirable book, *Sporting Days and Sporting Ways* (1910) social historian Ralph Nevil gives us a clear picture of the young Irish Corinthian at this formative stage of his life:

> Lord Waterford was a constant frequenter of the sporting hostelries of London, and at Limmer's conceived many of his wild jokes.
>
> The eccentricities of this nobleman were indeed numberless. He painted the Melton toll-bar a bright red, put aniseed on the hoofs of a parson's horse, and hunted the terrified divine with bloodhounds. On another occasion he put a donkey into the bed of a stranger at an inn.
>
> He took a hunting-box in the shires, and amused himself with shooting out the eyes of the family portraits with a pistol. He smashed a very valuable French clock on the staircase at Crockford's with a blow of his first, and solemnly proposed to one of the first railway companies in Ireland to start two engines in opposite directions on the same line in order that he might witness the smash, for which he proposed to pay.'

As I have already mentioned, the young Waterford was

very handy with his fists, and often went out with a group of acquaintances seeking fights with likely-looking tradesmen. Among his particular friends were Lord Methuen and Billy Duff, and Ralph Nevill tells us that 'the party was never so happy as when engaging butchers and draymen in fistic encounters.'

Lord Methuen was apparently a man of predigious physique, and in his day was reputed to have raised a fifteen-stone man from a table with one hand. The other member of this awesome trio, Billy Duff, was a lightweight, but of a square build and a very quick and capable boxer. He once fought a butcher almost twice his size in the middle of Pall Mall — the luckless man being deceived by Duff's appearance and thereby receiving a severe thrashing!

Waterford was also a skilled horseman 'daring to the verge of insanity' Nevill tells us, but unhappily needlessly cruel to his animals. He was further an accomplished sailor, as the same authority mentions in recounting another anecdote about the wild young nobleman.

> At times Lord Waterford was foolhardy almost beyond belief. On board his yacht, the *Charlotte*, in the Bay of Biscay, whilst it was blowing a gale, this scion of a mercurial stock happened to lose his cap, which was carried away by a gust of wind whilst he was on deck watching the sailors shorten sail.
>
> 'Hello,' said the captain, 'there's my tile gone; lower away the boat and send some men to get it.'
>
> 'My Lord,' respectfully urged his skipper, 'no boat could live in such a sea.'
>
> 'The deuce it can't,' was the rejoinder; 'then I'll see whether I can or not', and as he spoke he leapt from the taffrail into the seething waters. It was now no time for hesitation, and the captain at once caused a boat to be lowered, and went to attempt the rescue of his reckless master, who was eventually reached about a mile astern of the vessel in an exhausted condition, but clutching his cap!

Such was the extraordinary, and unsavoury, character of the young Marquis, that by the early months of 1836 his exploits were the subject of more than just gossip in the London sporting houses — the newspapers, too, began to take an interest in him. At first, it was the local and county papers which found his eccentricities worth reporting. On March 11, 1836, the *Stamford Mercury* carried the following item:

> The Marquis of Waterford whose pranks have frequently drawn him within the powerfully attractive influence of police stations in both the old and the new world, has been showing off at Melton Mowbray during the last week.
>
> After smashing several windows, and offering a bonus to some street passengers to fight with him, he turned his attention to a member of the medical profession, who is remarkable for his gentlemanly conduct and unoffending deportment, who happened to be riding up the street, and being near the turnpike gate, the noble marquis seized the bridle and peremptorily demanded the toll. The gentleman mildly replied to his rudeness by stating that he had already paid for going through the gate, and requested to be suffered quietly to proceed. Some blows hereupon were inflicted by his dignified assailant, and a certain epithet applied, too gross for utterance.
>
> It is stated that a note of apology has been forwarded to the insulted party, who, it is hoped, will refer the matter to the decision of the law, rather than by compromising so gross an outrage encourage a repetition of such conduct towards some who have neither spirit nor money to demand justice.

Whether the Marquis saw or cared about the reproof delivered in this report, it made not the slightest difference to his wildness. In April he was in trouble for leaving an old lady trapped in her overturned sedan chair, the *Bedford Chronicle* reported, and a month later a disapproving paragraph in the *Hertfordshire Mercury* accused him of starting an 'unseemly incident' at the local inn where he had got two servant girls drunk and made them fight him for the amusement of his friends. After defeating the befuddled females, the paper said, the Marquis had placed them across his knee and delivered a sound spanking to both 'for presuming that even two women were match enough for a man at any sport.'

These were, of course, rural escapades, and as such seemingly of little interest to the London papers. When the mighty *Times* chose to mention the Marquis a month later in June, it was in a completely different light — as if it felt somehow responsible for preserving the dignity of the nobility, even if they were inclined to go off the rails a little at times. The item in the paper of June 21 was headed simply, 'The Marquis of Waterford' and read:

> It is a pleasing duty to record a truly noble and humane act upon the part of this nobleman. A few days ago as his lordship was travelling in the neighbourhood of Kilsheenan, in Tipperary, he was struck with the appearance of a farmer's horse which his carriage overtook on the road. After a few preliminaries the animal changed owners, and became the property of the noble marquis.
>
> The farmer, however, elated, no doubt, by his ready sale, was resolved to show off the merits of the horse, but in doing so the animal became so restive and irritated that he broke to pieces the vehicle to which he was harnessed, and fractured the arm of the farmer, beside inflicting other injuries upon him.
>
> Upon witnessing the accident the Marquis of Waterford immediately left his carriage and, causing three gentlemen who were with him at the time to do the same, he had the sufferer placed within it, and drove with him to the house of a neighbouring gentleman, where he had every attention paid him. Not content with this, his Lordship, in the most generous manner, gave him £5, and returned him his horse. He further directed no expense to be spared, to have him removed to Clonmel, and to have the ablest surgeon there employed for him. He is now under the care of Dr Burgess and rapidly recovering. We will not add a word of comment.

Commendable as this action would seem to have been, *The Times* might well have weighed in the balance of its story, a report that the Marquis had only shortly before been responsible for abruptly turning 30 families off his land at Curraghmore. The local paper, the *Waterford Chronicle*, had reported on March 23, that the 'cruel and inhuman system of turning human beings on the high road' had been renewed by the agent of the Marquis. 'Upwards of 30 families,' it said, 'residing near the demesne of Curraghmore, have, within the last two days, received the usual order to turn out. The circumstances of the case to which we are referring shall claim our most serious attention, and if our information be justly founded, we shall make the Empire acquainted with the treatment which a population of 150 people are receiving from those who ought to be the first to protect them.'

The paper continued in similar vein and concluded, 'If

the country remains in profound tranquility, it will be easily admitted that we are by no means indebted for that blessing to the aristocracy, who, for their own selfish purposes, turn so many human beings adrift on the wide world. It is, however, our duty to watch over the interests of the community, and we pledge ourselves that no man, however elevated may be his station, shall, with impunity, carry on such a wholesale system of depopulation as that which has just commenced in the neighbourhood of Portlaw.'

But such blasts, even from his local paper, were not to distract the young and irresponsible Marquis from his life of pleasure. The estate was a matter for others until he was too old for the high life.

For the remainder of that year he continued to travel around the countryside and enjoy himself — but when he overstepped the mark yet again in the following April, 1837, even *The Times* could not pass the matter over. This time, too, there was no way the exploits could be hushed up with ready money, and in August the Marquis and a number of his friends appeared at the Derby Assizes.

The group, consisting of the Marquis, Sir Frederick Johnstone, the Hon. A.C.H. Villiers and E.H. Reynard Esq., were charged with causing a riot and assault. The events in question had occurred on April 5, the day of the Croxton Park Races, held about five miles from Melton Mowbray.

The four defendants, said the prosecution, had attended the races, and in the evening gone into Melton Mowbray to dine. At about two o'clock in the morning of the following day, the two town watchmen, on hearing a noise, proceeded to the market place. There, near Lord Roseberry's house, they saw several gentlemen attempting to overturn a caravan. As the watchmen drew closer they saw that there was a man inside the caravan who was considerably frightened.

The Times reported what it was alleged happened next:

> The watchmen succeeded in preventing the caravan being over-turned, at which the Marquis of Waterford challenged one of them to fight. The watchman declined.
>
> Subsequently hearing a noise in the direction of the toll-bar, the men proceeded thither, and found the gate-keeper had been

screwed up in his house, and he had been calling out 'Murder!'. On coming up with the gentlemen a second time, it was observed they had a pot of red paint with them, while one of them carried a paint brush, which one of the constables wrestled from the hand of the person who held it; but subsequently they surrounded the man, threw him on his back, and painted with red paint his face and neck.

They then continued their games, painting the doors and windows of different persons; and when one of their companions (Mr Reynard) was put in the lock-up, they forced the constable to give up the keys, and succeeded in getting him out.

The paper went on to report that various witnesses were called to positively identify the men, and report on the damage and distress which they had caused in the town. None of the defendents denied their action and all gave the appearance of being indifferent to the entire proceedings.

The jury withdrew for only a few moments and returned with a verdict of guilty of common assault against each man. The judge ordered a fine of £100 each, and added that they were to be held in prison if these were not immediately paid.

It comes as no surprise to read that the young hell-raisers were out of the Assize building within the hour and celebrating their 'freedom' shortly thereafter at the self-same inn where the evening of trouble had begun.

There was a sequel to this episode — though not as the law might have hoped, a change of heart against such outrageous behaviour by the Marquis. He was as determined as ever to continue his life of pleasure — but not in a district such as this one which failed to appreciate or tolerate his high-jinks.

A paragraph from the *Leamington Chronicle* of July 24 1837 tells all:

THE MARQUIS OF WATERFORD

In consequence of the late unpleasant circumstances at Melton Mowbray, in which the above named nobleman was said to be implicated, he and his friends are determined to remove their large establishments from Leicestershire, where they spent large sums of money annually, and in future to fix their headquarters at Leamington.

However, neither the citizens of Leamington, nor anywhere else in the British Isles for that matter, had any way of knowing that the Marquis was on the verge of the greatest 'prank' of his life.

Before fixing their headquarters in Leamington, the Marquis and his friends decided to shake the dust of England from their shoes for a while. They had become bored with the lack of variety in their lives, and felt that a change of climate might be good for them. Perhaps, also, their notoriety might not have gone before them and put a damper on any 'exploits' they planned.

At first they talked of the idea of an expedition to Africa, but the heat and discomfort that they would have to endure settled against this. The Marquis fancied a cruise, and so after further discussion it was agreed on sailing his yacht, the *Charlotte*, to Scandinavia. None of the men had visited these parts, and there were stories they had all heard of the beauty of Swedish and Norwegian girls. . .

So in the first week of August, the party of four men and their crew set sail in the yacht, making their first stop at Portsmouth for provisions. Thereafter they crossed the Channel and made stop-overs at several of the French coastal resorts before proceeding up the North Sea towards the Norwegian coast.

The days passed congenially enough, the young noblemen basking in the hot summer sun, drinking and occasionally engaging in not-too-strenuous deck games. The *Charlotte* made a brief stop at Stavanger and then after weaving through the scenic islands of the Hardangerfj, docked at Bergen on the morning of August 11.

By nightfall the Marquis was in trouble again — but this time he seemed rather less to blame than usual.

For their first evening's entertainment in the new city, the young bloods had gone to Hoffett's small public house in the district of Nostest. It had been recommended to them and indeed it was not long before they were in their usual high spirits and had talked three serving girls into joining their table for dinner.

The Marquis had taken a particular fancy to blonde, buxom Anne Uldenhoft, a bright-eyed and mischievous young woman. By eleven o'clock both were well on the way to being drunk and already talking in the most intimate terms.

Young Anne was naturally flattered at receiving the attentions of an Irish nobleman, and when a short while later he suggested they took a walk and she showed him some of the local beauty spots, she readily agreed.

Out in the fresh air, the two young people clung to each other for support and began to laugh. The Marquis placed his hat on the girl's head and then drew a bottle from his pocket. He put it to his mouth and when he tried to take a swig realised that the cork was still in. He burst into laughter again.

It was at this moment that a night watchman came striding out of the gloom and the light-hearted evening took a different turn altogether. In the records of the master of police at Bergen are details of the subsequent examination he carried out into the events of that night. In the light of later developments, the statements are worth reprinting in full:

> The first witness examined was the watchman Brynild Larsen Hamre, forty-four years of age, who deposed, that while on his post at the Halvkand Height, at eleven o'clock in the evening of the 11th instant, he had heard loud vociferations down in the New-way.
>
> On the other side of the hill he met a woman with a man's hat on, and by her side a man without a hat. Hearing that the man, who was dressed in a white smock-frock, was a stranger, he (the watchman) ordered the woman to be quiet. They paid no attention to his remonstrance, and the stranger stooped, lifted up a stone, and advanced towards him.
>
> He wished to make the stranger incapable of mischief by giving him a smart blow on the right arm; but, as the latter stooped at the moment to catch hold of him, the blow unintentionally came upon the head, and the stranger fell.
>
> The fire officer on duty, Mr Albert Mohn, a merchant, said he had come up on hearing the blow given, and seeing a man fall. The watchman appeared to him to be sober, but the Englishman seemed to be intoxicated.
>
> The morning star used on this occasion was a stick with an iron spike at one end, and a bullet at the other; it was the latter end

that the watchman struck, and the bullet was broken off by the blow.

Also examined was Anne Catherine Uldenhoft, twenty-three years of age, who resided with two other girls at the public house of Hoffett, in Nostest.

On the 11th instant, six or seven Englishmen came to the house, and one of them had gone out with her to take a walk over the New-way about eleven o'clock. He had put his hat on her head before leaving the house. He took a bottle out of his pocket and put it to his mouth, but observing that the cork was still in it, he burst into a loud laugh.

At that moment the watchman came up, abused them for making a noise, and, with his morning star, struck the Englishman on his back, at which the latter laughed louder than before. They then went over the Halvkands Height, passing the watchman, but, as the Englishman continued to laugh out aloud, she was not able to get away from him until the watchman came up and struck him a blow, which threw him on the ground.

From these witnesses' reports a somewhat confused picture emerges. The seemingly acquiesent serving girl suddenly talks about wanting to 'get away' from her escort and could not do so until the watchman had beaten him to the ground. And did the drunken Marquis pick up a stone — only the watchman says so — and was the custodian of the law justified in hitting him, possibly twice, and so hard?

In any event, the other members of the Marquis's party lodged a complaint the following day with the British Consul about his treatment, and a doctor's report on Waterford's injuries shows him to have been badly beaten. This again can be turned up in the Bergen police office:

Dr A. Heiberg, town-physician, deposed on the 16th, that the blow had fallen on the right temple, and had inflicted a wound which had pierced to the bone. A considerable swelling and discolouring of the skin ensued subsequently, extending over the whole temple and eyelid. Nearer to the cranium were two superficial wounds of no importance. The blow must have been struck with extraordinary force, and had occasioned so severe a concussion of the brain that the Marquis's life was still in danger. On the back there was no mark of a blow having been given; but on the loins there is a round blue spot of the size of a dollar, evidently occasioned by some external act of violence. The farther examination was then adjourned till his lordship's recovery.

Indeed his Lordship's recovery was to take nearly a month — hardly, one would have thought, the amount of time necessary for an injury allegedly sustained by a light blow on a man renowned for his strength. The incident, however, did more than wound the Marquis; it also hurt his pride deeply — the more so when the local newspapers praised the watchman for his actions.

'The well-known Marquis of Waterford has attempted to play the pranks in our streets by which he has acquired a very equivocal reputation in the United Kingdom,' wrote the *Bergen Morgenavisen*, 'but unhappily encountered a watchman who is one of the most vigorous of our guardians of the night, and a blow of whose staff felled the Marquis to the ground, whence he was taken up half dead.'

The cruise to Scandinavia had now turned sour for Waterford. Although recovered, he was depressed and in a foul temper. No one in the party dared to argue when he said that the *Charlotte* was to return home immediately.

On September 18, the yacht docked in Aberdeen, and the *Caledonian Mercury* reported that the party 'left next day for the south'. The Marquis seemed to be in better spirits, the paper added, and for a while nothing was heard of him.

Then in the last week of October, the *Fife Herald* carried a small item which apparently indicated that he was back at all his old tricks again. *The Times* reprinted the story in its issue of Friday, October 17:

> KINROSS — The Marquis of Waterford passed through this town the other day, on the top of a coach, with a few of his associates. In the course of the journey they amused themselves with the noble occupation of popping eggs from a basket at any individual who happened to be standing at the wayside. *Fife Herald*. (This vivacious person is a long time sowing his 'wild oats'. He is nearly 27 years old.)

Two days later there was a completely unexpected development. For the first time, a report about his activities was contradicted by the Marquis. On the Monday morning, October 30, *The Times* carried the following retraction:

> We are desired to contradict the statement which appeared in our paper on Friday last. . . we are authorised to say that the noble Marquis is at present, and has been for some weeks past, confined by illness at his residence in London, and, consequently, could not have been a party to the transaction referred to in the *Fife Herald*.

It is strange that of all the stories about him, the Marquis should have chosen to deny this one. For he was certainly not confined to his residence but had, in fact, attended several public functions in October as the social columns of the *London Gazette* reveal. But what it does clearly establish from the point of view of this book, is that he was in London when the activities of Spring Heeled Jack began.

I have also discovered in the *Memoirs and Correspondence* of Waterford's friend and fellow-prankster, Sir Frederick Johnstone, privately published in 1858, a few important lines concerning the Marquis's return journey from Bergen to London.

> 'On the coach journey from Scotland,' says Sir Frederick, 'there were many efforts on the part of his friends to raise Henry's spirits. He evinced the most bitter hatred of the police authorities for their part in the matter and talked in the most depreciating terms of the servant girl whom, he said, was in part to blame. Try as we could to distract his mind to other things he kept to the subject as if the night watchman's blows had somehow affected his reason. Only when the talk was of new wagers did he show any interest, and I believe his later return to good spirits *was due to a daring venture the others proposed for his return to London.*'

What a tantalising reference — but unfortunately Sir Frederick, who naturally later in his life was a little reticent about his spirited youth, says no more of the matter. Yet certain basic ingredients are undeniably there: the still incensed Marquis, furious with the law authorities, and in particular with a girl whom he felt was partly to blame for his pain and indignity. Could this man with his particular temperament have resisted a wager to get even with such people, albeit by proxy, if as Sir Frederick hints, such a wager was offered him?

If we examine the evidence we learn that during the

winter months the Marquis stayed a day or two with a number of friends dwelling in large houses around the environs of London — a factor which closely allies with the statement made in the previous chapter that Spring Heeled Jack 'seemed to base himself on private parks, resting a few days in each.'

In particular we know that he stayed at the curious building known as 'Vanbrugh Castle' on Maze Hill, Blackheath at the time of the 'hog and pleasure' fair, October 11, when, as you will recall, the terrible attack on the servant girl, Polly Adams, occured. We know also that he visited the fair during the course of the day because there is a report in the *London Gazette* that 'a party lead by the Marquis of Waterford desported themselves with much merriment at Blackheath Fair', and Polly's description of the 'nobleman with pop eyes' who first laid hands on her as she walked among the stalls is strikingly like Waterford.

The man's peculiar ringing laughter, which Polly heard again when attacked by Spring Heeled Jack, is another feature the Marquis possessed, as the woman who later became his wife, Louisa, Marchioness of Waterford, remarks in one of her letters which is reprinted by Augustus J. Hare in his book, *The Story of Two Noble Lives* (1893).

The Times of this winter period also offers another piece in the jigsaw, for it disclosed on Friday, November 24 that the Marquis was reported to be indisposed 'arising from a complaint of the eyes'. More than one doctor whom I have consulted, has agreed that any man utilising a flaming material close to his eyes as Spring Heeled Jack did — particularly a man with protuberant eyes — would almost certainly have suffered some kind of eye inflammation after a period of time. And it is notable that at the period of this *Times* report there are no records of the agile terror of London being seen.

Of crucial importance, too, is the evidence of Mr Ashworth's servant boy who was confronted by Spring Heeled Jack and noticed the gold filigree letter 'W' on the man's cloak. This matches with descriptions of Waterford's emblem and in the light of the other evidence, seems more than mere coincidence.

If, then, I may be allowed my conviction that Henry,

Marquis of Waterford, was Spring Heeled Jack, why did he create the bizarre disguise? And, more important, how did he manage to elude capture?

We shall probably never know quite what inspired him to devise the flaming features, flowing cloak and springs-in-the-heels which made up the terror of London, though it would seem to be modelled on the traditional idea of the Devil — or some kind of demon — and therefore immediately inspire certain deeply-rooted fears. It was an undeniably original concept, and certainly guaranteed to terrify anyone who saw it.

Although I believe some of the descriptions of his leaps and bounds are exaggerated by fright, I think he did possess concealed springs in his boots which enabled him to travel with extra speed when making his getaway.

It has been suggested to me — and I find the theory most plausible — that the springs may have been made of an alloy of steel and another metal which would effectively double the elasticity of the steel and at the same time halve its weight. They would probably have had to be at least 18 inches long when fully extended to permit leaps of any great distance.

The springs were almost certainly attached to a thin metal plate in the shape of the sole of the boot and secured by metal uprights firmly affixed by screws and laces in a stout leather gaiter which was shaped to the wearer's leg from ankle to knee. This would, of course, be necessary to give the wearer balance and control over the springs — and the appearance of such equipment, looking very much like tall leather boots in the half light, explains how the most common description of them arose.

Apart from his own ingenuity, Waterford also had several former university friends who had studied mathematics and applied mechanics at Oxford while he was there, and with whom he socialised in London, who would have been only too delighted to help him devise the 'spring heeled boots' for such a devilish scheme.

I think, too, that he avoided capture by a mixture of instilling such fear into those who saw him that the last thing they thought about was grappling with the monster, and the aid of at least one dedicated accomplice. I cannot believe he could have carried out some of his most daring exploits without somebody nearby with a coach to whisk him away immediately afterwards, suitably changed into ordinary day clothes. The evidence that somebody returned to the scene of the attack on Jane Alsop outside her home in East London to pick up the cloak which Jack had thrown down, is undisputed.

Waterford, as we have seen, was never short of friends to join in his 'pranks' and didn't the Spring Heeled Jack episode just involve more brutal and daring exploits of the kind they had so often undertaken in the past? Any one of the gentlemen I have already named as his friends might have aided him in the attacks — indeed all may have done so at various times — and it would obviously be as much in their own interests as his not to say anything afterwards.

We know, too, that the Marquis had friends in high places: and although I cannot accept the idea that there was a 'conspiracy of silence' among the press and authorities to keep the story of Spring Heeled Jack quiet, there is no doubt that if there was suspicion that the villain of the peace might be a nobleman or some person of high estate, it was not something anyone at that time with a job to protect might want to be responsible for uncovering. And, as the records show, Waterford, for all his wildness, was an intimate of Court circles, a member of the Royal Yacht Squadron, and in 1841 was actually offered the Mastership of Queen Victoria's staghounds.*

* *The Kelso Warder* reported on September 16, 1841: 'At the suggestion of HRH Prince Albert, and to the no small delight of his grace, the Duke of Wellington, Sir Robert Peel offered the mastership of Her Majesty's stag hounds to the Marquis of Waterford, who declined the honour. 'Prince Albert and you,' he said, 'are d- - - d good fellows, but neither of you could see which way a Tipperary man went across country. I am pledged to Her Majesty's sporting subjects in that part of the United Kingdom, and I am too much attached to them to repeal the union and cordiality that subsists between us. If his Royal Highness would honour us with his presence, I will ensure him good sport and a hearty welcome in every habitation from Jemmy Millett's to my own, and I'll mount him on a good 'un and no mistake.' If the reader accepts my belief that Waterford was Spring Heeled Jack, he will need no reminding of the irony of the situation that the Duke of Wellington should have been delighted at the proposal. For this was the very man the Duke had unknowingly rode out, pistols in hand, to try and capture! Sir Robert Peel, too, had indirectly tried to hunt him down through the unavailing efforts of his police force!

In one of the few published articles on the legend of Spring Heeled Jack, Elliott O'Donnell (who earned something of a reputation as a 'ghost hunter' and published numerous books about hauntings) said he was not convinced that the Marquis was Spring Heeled Jack, but almost certainly knew who he was. In *Haunted Britain* (1948) he wrote:

> 'It was thought at the time that the Marquis of Waterford, whose wild doings were constantly reported in the newspapers, was probably acquainted with the identity of the mysterious nocturnal assailant of women. Some thought that if that being was not the Marquis himself, it was one of his associates.'

After noting that the *Annual Register* for May 1838 thought that his eccentricities 'arose more from a natural defect of mind than from any cause for which he can be held more directly responsible', O'Donnell sums up: 'In none of his recorded vagaries and misdeeds would he appear to have been guilty of any such cruelty to women as characterised the acts of Spring Heeled Jack. As proof that he could not have been Spring Heeled Jack, that being has been seen, periodically, for the last hundred years.'

I am afraid, however, that the evidence I have presented shows Waterford to have been cruel to women as well as men, and we have heard how cruel he could be to his horses. Certainly his 'pranks' were often unnecessarily vicious and inconsiderate towards his fellow humans. In short, there was behind what was tolerantly described as high spirits, a very real sadistic streak. Lastly, to say that as 'proof' he could not have been Spring Heeled Jack because the agile terror has been seen ever since is no proof at all. It merely indicates, as I shall show, that others took up the successful disguise for their own ends.

It is also my conviction that after the incident with the servant boy the Marquis either lost interest in his persona or was urged by his friends to give up the exploits before he was caught. Perhaps he suspected he might already have left behind some clues, and with the widescale hunt on for Jack, a path could eventually lead to him because of his renowned wildness. He must also have been well aware of the fact that several people had been arrested on suspicion of

The Marquis of Waterford as an older man, settled in Ireland.

being the terror, and although all had been released after questioning, the net might well be closing.

Or perhaps most simply of all, he had won his wager. He had terrorised London, worked out his fury at the police authorities by resisting all their efforts to catch him, and enjoyed the excitement of an unparalleled and outrageous 'prank'.

Although, of course, there will always be the element of doubt, my case is, I think, further strengthened by the fact that one famous contemporary was quite convinced of the Marquis's involvement in the birth of Spring Heeled Jack — that doyen of the literary world, the Reverend E. Cobham Brewer, compiler of the famous 'Reader's Handbook'.*

---

* Another item confirming the identification is to be found in the prestigious magazine, *Notes & Queries* for September 28, 1907, under the heading 'Marquis of Waterford as Spring Heeled Jack.' Mr Harry Hems of Fair Park, Exeter writes, 'My maternal grandmother who died at an advanced age in 1850, was accustomed to tell me, when I was a little lad, uncanny stories about Spring Heeled Jack, who, she asserted, was believed to be one Marquis of Waterford. The monster was credited with hiding at night in dark and lonely places, and when some chance pedestrian came along (by preference a solitary female) Spring Heeled Jack would suddenly jump out at one bound and pin his unlucky victim to the ground.'

The Reverend Cobham, of Edwinstowe Vicarage in Newark, devoted his life to his handbook and amassed a wealth of first-hand material about folk lore and legends. Under the heading 'Spring Heeled Jack' he wrote with absolute conviction:

> SPRING HEELED JACK. The Marquis of Waterford, in the early part of the 19th Century, used to amuse himself by springing on travellers unawares, to terrify them; and from time to time others have followed his silly example.

And what of the Marquis after this period? There were a few more 'pranks'* but these grew infrequent and by 1840 he was apparently a much more settled person, becoming increasingly involved in the management of his estates at Curraghmore. When he married Louisa Rothesay, the daughter of Lord Stuart de Rothesay, in June 1842, the transformation was complete.

In his biography of Louisa, *The Story of Two Noble Lives*, Augustus Hare writes of their meeting with an obvious desire to minimise the transgressions of the past: 'Henry, third Marquis of Waterford, noble in heart and appearance, had been known in his youth as the 'wild Lord Waterford', and his many strange exploits, not one of which was unworthy of a chivalrous gentleman, were the subject of a thousand stories. Entirely devoted to hunting and sport, he might naturally be thought to have little in common with

---

* The last publicised 'incident' I have been able to trace in which he features was reported in *The Times* of May 3, 1838. It was headed 'Marquis of Waterford's Patronage' and read: 'At a meeting of Middlesex Magistrates on Tuesday, the Landlord of the 'Turk's Head' in the Haymarket, appealed against the refusal of four magistrates to renew the licence of the house. Mr Phillips, who appeared for the respondents, said he would show the sort of patronage the Marquis of Waterford, of whom he wished to speak with every respect, had extended to the house in question. The noble Marquis had ordered a butt of sherry wine to be given away at the house, and the qualification for the recipients was that they should be women of abandoned character. The learned counsel described the scene that ensued after the distribution of the sherry; and called witnesses, who proved that the house was a complete scene of riot during the time the wine was being distributed, and that a body of police were obliged to interfere. The 'noble' Marquis was present on the occasion and had a fight with a man in the house. The police interrupted the fight, and dispersed the crowd. The appeal was, of course, instantly quashed.'

the *spirituelle* art-loving daughter of Lord Stuart de Rothesay. But from the moment when her glorious beauty flashed upon him at the Eglinton tournament, he was her devoted knight and only lived to win her. His extreme shyness and diffidence, however, made him shrink from a proposal, till his sister had written to her mother.'

From hell-raiser to diffident lover in one stroke! As the *Waterford News* reported later with perhaps more object-ivity, 'Forgetting all his past as if it were a dream, Lord Waterford entered hand in hand with his wife into all her schemes for ameliorating the wretchedness by which they were surrounded, and their efforts were ever crowned with success.'

But this blissful state of affairs was not to last — tragedy struck Lady Waterford that same year when she was flung from her horse and, for several days, hovered near death. Fortunately, she recovered with no ill-effects, but the passion for riding was to take a fatal toll of her husband. He was to die in an accident close to the same spot.

Writing in his *Memoirs of an Ex-Minister* (1884), the Earl of Malmesbury, who was Foreign Secretary during Lord Grey's Premiership, and a family friend, notes that on March 29th 1859, 'Lord Waterford was killed out hunting, near Curraghmore. His horse stumbled over a small fence, and, falling on his head, Lord Waterford dislocated his neck — a singular death for a man who had had so many escapes.'

It was, indeed, a cruel twist of fate that the man who had been that master of agility, Spring Heeled Jack, should have died this way. But the legend which he had begun was not to go to the grave with him. Already it was growing still larger and moving beyond the confines of London.

Spring Heeled Jack was next to become a national prob-lem — and murder was to be added to the other crimes already attributed to his name. . .

5

The Agile Murderer

Although it is my belief that the Marquis of Waterford created and used the disguise of Spring Heeled Jack during the Winter and Spring of 1837-8, thereafter turning to other things, it was far from the end of the story. The persona of this agile terror had so caught the imagination of prankster and criminal alike that there was not long to wait before he bounded from the shadows again.

Of course, there is little doubt that there were stories going around even during the rest of 1838 that Spring Heeled Jack was active. But these we can feel certain were pure figments of the imagination. It is quite easy to appreciate how in London, at least, the reign of terror that the mystery man had inspired left a mark on the minds of every susceptible man and woman in the capital. Just as top-hatted policemen had been set upon during the height of the panic, now many an innocent figure or innocuous shape suddenly took on the appearance of the mysterious Jack in suspicious minds.

The police, for their part, were highly relieved when the weeks began to pass after the attacks in Bow and Limehouse, not forgetting the encounter in Commerical Road, and nothing further of any substance was heard about this callous and mysterious criminal. During the previous months they had hauled in for questioning quite a considerable number of suspects, but all their endeavours had lead to nothing.

The masked attacker had slipped through their fingers with all the agility for which he was now famous. In truth, there was not a sergeant or police constable from one side of London to the other who was not heartily sick of the name of Spring Heeled Jack and did not utter a silent prayer that he had departed the scene for good.

There were those in the immediate aftermath who tried to put the whole matter down to hallucination: that the stories were all imagination and that nobody had been really attacked at all. This of course ignored the evidence of frightened girls who still had the marks of Jack's claws vividly scratched across their skins. And there were others who picked up discrepancies in the stories of those who had been attacked and sought logical explanations for the so-called feats of Jack.

There were suggestions from some quarters that the girls had invented the attacks to cover up illicit activities of their own. An attacker who left marks over female flesh was an ideal excuse for a girl who had succumbed, perhaps reluctantly, to the attentions of her lover and then panicked at the possible reaction of her parents. What could be simpler than to say she had been attacked by the mystery man? But as we have seen in our study of the major reports, there is not one such hypothesis which stands up to much examination.

Not everyone was afraid of Spring Heeled Jack, however. There were small sections of the London population who saw him as a kind of Robin Hood — a bold, exciting figure who cared nothing for the law and took what was his fancy. Given the sadistic way in which he treated his victims, this is not a view that is easy to subscribe to; but in the harder times of early Victorian England not entirely difficult to understand.

Those who lived in the rarified heights of society and only took the vaguest interest in what went on outside the gossip of their circles, felt that Jack must be a lunatic and left it at that. It was perhaps an appropriate, if not sound, viewpoint, for at that time a newly constituted Commission on Lunacy was just beginning its sittings in London!

Not surprisingly, there were differences of opinion about the appearance of Spring Heeled Jack. The flowing cloak, the vicious clawed hands and leaping heels were common to

Spring Heeled Jack as a 'Robin Hood' figure, terrorising an evil nobleman in a 'Penny Dreadful' serial.

all the accounts — but there were some varying ideas about his face. The eyes of fire and the flames which leapt from the mouth were almost universal, but the idea that he wore a face-covering of some kind persisted, too. A few witnesses believed he had some kind of helmet that enveloped his head, and this, as we shall see in a later chapter, has become one of the cornerstones to the theory that Jack might have been a man from another planet.

Whatever the exact disguise consisted of, it seems most probable to me that it was a mask which covered the face from hairline to chin and was made of a metal which prevented the fire and flames from scalding the wearer's skin. The flames which leapt from the mouth are easily explained — the technique of the fire eater who could blow flames from his mouth was well enough known in 1837 and the trick not hard to learn by an educated and resourceful man. The fiery eyes were probably made to appear so by the flames and this effect would be enhanced by a man with large, protubent eyes like the Marquis of Waterford. It is also interesting to recall at this point Spring Heeled Jack's request for a candle before attacking Jane Alsop in Bow; obviously the assistant, or assistants, who probably accompanied him, could have supplied the initial light he required on other occasions.

The actual bounds which Jack took — and which grew in height and distance as the legend developed — were, as I have already indicated, exaggerated, although compressed springs hidden in the heels of the boots did make him lighter and swifter on his feet than ordinary men.

Such, in my view, was the equipment of the first Spring Heeled Jack — a clever combination of fright-maker and agility aid. It was a concept too original and effective to be left dormant for long.

As far as I have been able to trace the next appearance of Spring Heeled Jack took place in the early 1840's. The accounts are, however, far from clear and much of the earliest evidence is based on oral records.

The first established reports came from the Home Counties where, in 1843, a 'cloaked being who breathed fire' assaulted a number of travellers on lonely roads. This same year a group of children in Surrey ran panic-stricken home to their parents with tales of a man 'with terrible eyes' who leapt over them as they walked home from school, and several women complained that a being 'like a devil on springs' had chased them along rural footpaths in Kent.

It seems to have taken little time for everyone to agree that Spring Heeled Jack was back on the prowl. He was certainly as light on his feet as ever, but the vicious claws now seemed to be missing.

Perhaps the most intriguing of these early reports is the one which appeared in *Lloyd's Penny Weekly Miscellany* for August 26 1843. It is headed ATTACK BY NIGHT and I have reproduced it in full below:

'As poor Jack B- - - - was returning to his residence in the Commercial Road, about midnight, he was met by a man, with a black, Spanish-made cloak over him, and a mask before his face. On passing, he turned and came after Jack: a struggle ensued, and the demon was beat off, but he returned to the charge with all the appearance of an intention to destroy Jack.

After a severe contest, on falling, the foot of the fiend was perceived to be cloven. Jack now made off with as much speed as he was able, being much fatigued and bruised with the blows received in defending himself from the Devilskin.

He soon made after Jack, and coming at him again with fresh fury, fortunately Jack gave him a blow which knocked him into the ditch against the mud-wall, which came to the Commercial Road, by the Hackney Fields.

He laid there for a moment, when he jumped up, and ran towards Jack, squeezed his body against Jack's, breathed flames and in a moment Jack was on fire. He then let go his hold, and jumped upon the mud-wall, on quitting the top of which, he turned round, and said he had done for poor Jack at last.

Jack's domicile being near, he got to it with much difficulty, and a medical man was procured, who long attended poor Jack before convalescence took place. The medical gentleman can vouch for the truth of this statement; indeed, poor Jack is still pained from the affair.'

The Commercial Road again! But this is certainly a very different kind of man to the one who knocked on Mr Ashworth's door in February 1838!

The following year reports began to be received from a still wider area. A man in a mask with whitened features was for several weeks said to be leaping out on young girls in Northamptonshire, while a figure 'the very image of the devil himself with horns and eyes of flame' ran riot on the highways of Hampshire. And in East Anglia, along the roads to the coast, the creature made a habit of springing before the mail coaches and terrifying the drivers. For a while numbers of these drivers refused to travel the routes, and even the addition of a guard carrying a gun did not assuage their fears. As one driver was reported to have said, 'That Spring Heeled Jack don't feel no ordinary bullet. You just can't stop 'im.'

Perhaps because, with rare exceptions, Jack stayed well clear of London during this new period of activity, his exploits failed to receive anything like the publicity they had enjoyed during the winter of 1837-8. His path criss-crossed the countryside from the Midlands to the South Coast, and though he was being reported at locations many miles distant at virtually the same time, it is doubtful whether the people at the time believed there was more than one such creature. But publicity or not, there could be no denying that he was now something of a legend throughout the country.*

In Chichester, to take a typical example, the Reverend E. Cobham Brewer reports in his *Reader's Handbook,* 'the neighbourhood was full of tales of this adventurer, and caused quite a little panic. Many nervous people were afraid to venture out after sunset for fear of being "sprung" upon.'

Elliot O'Donnell, the 'ghost hunter' I have mentioned previously, also had a story which was similar to many others being repeated across a wide area of England at this time. He recounts it in his book, *Haunted Britain.*

'Spring Heeled Jack was a most ubiquitous being,' he says by way of preface. 'At one time he was scaring the Eastern and Southern Counties, while, at another, he was doing the same thing in the Midlands. In the forties he was particularly active in various parts of England.'

---

* As Elizabeth Villiers has commented in her book, *Stand & Deliver*: "All over the country, not in London alone, practical jokers, wearing cloaks and masks, leaped out of dark corners to kiss girls, and sometimes such jokers added robbery to assault, but these were imitators of the real Spring Heeled Jack and were far behind him in the mystery with which he was connected."

Mr O'Donnell then goes on to describe a story he was told as a child:

> I well remember my old nurse telling me of an experience she once had with him in Herefordshire. She was walking one evening with her aunt along a lonely country road in the neighbourhood of her home.
>
> The moon was full and, in its light, objects in the landscape stood out, with quite wonderful distinctness. The dark shadows of the trees and of the hedges lay clearly defined on the roadside. Hardly a breath of wind stirred.
>
> My nurse and her companion were approaching a slight dip in the road, when a tall figure, wearing some very fantastic garment, came soaring over the hedge on one side of them, and landing noiselessly in the middle of the road a few yards in front, with a mighty bound, leapt over the high hedge on the other side of them. They were far too terrified to see what became of the strange jumper after that.
>
> I asked my old nurse if it was man or woman, and she said, 'It was neither. How could it be? No human being could have bounded over hedges like that thing had done.' Her aunt told her it was Spring Heeled Jack, who had recently been terrifying country folk by bounding over walls and haystacks at night.

Mr O'Donnell adds that Jack was also 'particularly active about that time in Worcestershire, Warwickshire and Staffordshire.' He believes that there were also periodical reports of his reappearances in these same counties and elsewhere in the fifties, sixties and seventies.

These memories of Jack's widespread activities were also shared by a regular contributor to that august journal, *Notes & Queries*, who signed himself 'St Swithin'. Writing in the issue of March 30 1907, he said, 'This active gentleman was one of the bugbears of the nineteenth century forties, and I remember that we heard of him in our Lincolnshire nursery.' The contributor added that there was always a great deal of controversy going on about his agility, and with a touch of humour he concludes, 'I believe I was inclined to confuse him with the owner of the seven league boots!'

This note about Jack stirred up memories among other contributors to the journal and further details about his activities in this period were soon forthcoming.

Mr Thomas Ratcliffe of Worksop, in the issue of May 18, 1907 wrote:

> He was a bugbear into and past the fifties, for at various spots in the Midlands this nimble-heeled gentleman had played his jumping pranks, to the frightening of people out of their wits — an easy matter enough with some; in fact Jack jumped and was seen in the imagination of many folk.
>
> About the end of the forties I had, I may say, a wholesome dread of meeting 'Jumping Jack' and seeing him bound.

Mr Ratcliffe went on to discuss a new element in the character of Jack — that he was now a persecutor of evil-doers. He writes:

> There was a good deal of interest in the why and wherefore of Jack's jumping, and how he managed his marvellous flights through the air. His jumps were intended to frighten evil-doers and frustrate their intentions. He was looked upon as a sort of Robin Hood. Various theories were suggested to explain his supposed methods of jumping, the one which found most favour being that underneath the heels of his jack boots were compressed springs, which when released afforded propulsion enough to send Jack yards high in any direction.

It was becoming clear at this time that as well as variances in his character, Jack's abilities were undoubtedly being utilised by more than one person. A Mr William Jaggard writing in the same issue of *Notes & Queries* throws some particularly interesting light on this new factor in the story:

> In Warwickshire Spring Heeled Jack became a terror in lonely country districts. On dark nights a youth, in ghostly disguise of mask and long white sheet, secreted himself behind hedges abutting on the highway near churchyards.
>
> His shoes were fitted with powerful and noiseless springs, enabling him to leap hedgerows with ease in case of pursuit. On the approach of a lonely wayfarer the 'ghost' suddenly appeared.
>
> After several women and children had been nearly shocked to death a hunt for the culprit was organised. He was eventually captured, and found to be the son of a local coal-merchant, a

youth not overburdened with common sense.

In Berkshire, some time before this, a similar foolhardy escapade cost a relative of mine her sanity for life through shock.

Mr Jaggard's letter, apart from demonstrating the multiplicity of Jacks that were now about, also indicated the growing danger the exploits were proving not only to reason, but life as well. However irresponsibly and viciously he behaved, I believe that it had never been the intention of Waterford as the original Spring Heeled Jack to kill anyone; merely to attack and frighten them. And indeed these later imitators were probably not seeking the death of their victims, either. But gambling with the effects of fright upon the heart, particularly of the old, is always a risk, and a death resulting from one of these attacks always seemed a probability.

And so it proved in 1845. To be fair, this first death attributed to Spring Heeled Jack was only indirectly his responsibility; yet it underlined the fear that his name engendered in people's minds at the time.

The case came to light at an inquest held at Yarmouth in Norfolk in September, 1845. Under a heading, 'CURIOUS CHARGE OF MURDER AT YARMOUTH', *The Illustrated London News* of September 27 began its report, 'An inquest took place on Monday at Yarmouth, before Mr Ferrier, the town Coroner, on the body of a man named Purdy. The case was one of a most extraordinary character, it being supposed that he came by his death in an affray with a young man of the name of Noble, while impersonating the mysterious "Spring Heeled Jack".'

During the evidence it was stated that the deceased, Thomas Purdy, was a man of fifty who for several days prior to his death had been confined to bed with pleurisy and inflamation of the lungs. On Saturday evening, his wife, who had been sitting up with him for several nights, finally fell asleep from extreme fatigue.

Shortly after midnight, said the paper, the unfortunate Purdy woke up and climbed out of bed. He was in a state of delirium, and imagined that one of his donkeys had got loose. When he left the room, his sleeping wife heard nothing.

82

Clad only in his shirt, the man stumbled out into his yard searching for the stables. In his confusion and the darkness he missed these buildings altogether and began feeling around the shutters of a neighbouring house.

At this point, the Coroner was told, the female occupant of the house caught sight of the strange white figure scrabbling at her windows and began screaming for assistance. At the sound of her shrieks, a young man named Henry Noble who had been passing on his way home, came running up.

'Thinking that it was a spree of a certain Spring Heeled Jack who had been terrifying the neighbourhood of late with his wild pranks,' says the newspaper account, 'he proceeded to inflict severe punishment upon the deceased, who died on the following day.'

Following Purdy's death, Noble, who worked for an engineer in Yarmouth, was arrested and charged with murder. However, the surgeon who made a post mortem examination on the body of the deceased, said that it was his opinion that death was not induced by the blows, or even accelerated by them. It had been brought about entirely by internal disease.

The report concluded, 'Noble was examined before the Mayor, but on the Coroner's jury returning a verdict of "Natural Death" he was discharged.'

It was a sad and sorry case and there was no denying the spectre of Spring Heeled Jack hanging over it, even if he had not been directly involved. He was, though, personally to blame for the events which took place on Jacob's Island, Bermondsey in November 1845.

Jacob's Island, one of the running sores on the face of London at this time, had been immortalised in 1838 by Charles Dickens in *Oliver Twist*. In fact, before Dickens' graphic portrait of this huddle of decaying slum houses infested with pestilence and inhabited by the scum of London, it was virtually unknown to Londoners. It was here that Fagin and his associates dwelt, and in reality the vice and corruption that went on there almost beggared description.

In the filthy, tumble-down houses, linked by crazy wooden galleries across stinking ditches, dwelt a motley assembly of watermen, costermongers, woodchoppers and all manner of petty thieves and criminals. 'These people,' says a report in the *Morning Chronicle* of 1837, 'are generally of the lowest class, and being congregated together, young and old they corrupt one another. It has, for a long time, been a thriving nursery for immorality. . . Drunkeness is the predominant vice in the district, not only with men, but equally with women.'

Jacob's Island was obviously not a place which many Londoners cared to visit — which makes Spring Heeled Jack's escapade there on a winter evening all the more bizarre.

For on the night of November 12, the traditionally cloaked and fire-breathing figure of Jack was seen jumping across the rotting galleries of Jacob's Island, and leaping over all those who crossed his path. Even the hardened villains and gin-soaked women of this den of vice took fright at the sight of the 'devil figure' and fled into their ramshackle dwellings.

But as he leaped from one side of the island to another, Jack paused on the bridge across the appropriately named Folly Ditch, cornering a bedraggled young prostitute of 13-years-old named Maria Davis who was about to set out to earn a few pence.

The ragged, wretched girl, who possessed a certain beauty under the grime and filth that covered her, stood rooted to the spot as Jack bounded up. He took one look at her, grasped her by the shoulders, and breathed fire into her face.

Huddled behind their windows, the few eye-witnesses said Jack picked the terrified girl up in his arms and with one jerk hurled her into the foul, muddy waters below. With a laugh, he then bounded over the bridge and was lost in the maze of buildings.

The poor girl cried out unavailingly as the oozing mud inexorably claimed her. But there was nothing anyone could do.

Later on, when the facts were reported to the police, the ditch was dragged and the girl's body recovered. Her death was recorded at the subsequent inquest as due to 'misadventure' — but the sullen and secretive inhabitants of Jacob's Island knew that she had been the first recorded

Recovering the body of the prostitute Maria Davis from Folly Ditch.

victim of Spring Heeled Jack.

I have, during the course of my researches, come across other references to killings which have been attributed to Spring Heeled Jack. There is the suggestion that a man found dead by the roadside in Surrey in 1848 'with claw marks across his face and body' was a victim of the terror: but there are also stories at this time of a wild animal having escaped from a circus at Croydon and I find this a more believable explanation of the man's death.

In Hertford in 1855, the body of a pretty young girl was found with burn marks on her legs and scratches across her shoulders and breasts, and she, too, was thought for a while to have encountered the agile assailant. Later a local man confessed that when she had resisted his advances he had killed her and made a half-hearted effort to burn her corpse.

Less clearly detailed is the story of an old woman found by a roadside in Middlesex in 1863 with such fear written across her face that she could only have been frightened to death by a terrifying attacker. And who more natural to blame than Jack — though there are no hard facts to justify such a conclusion.*

And so I could go on with several more mysterious killings loosely attributed to Jack which do not really stand the test of thorough examination. In the end, I am only satisfied that the murder of the young prostitute can be definitely attributed to our legendary criminal.

As the nineteenth century drew on into its last quarter and gas lighting and the other new trappings of the rapidly developing and increasingly more sophisticated society began to drive superstition into the farthest corners of Queen Victoria's realm, the stories of Spring Heeled Jack became fewer. This, I hasten to add, is not to imply that previously they had been only the result of superstition, but rather that there had been plenty emanating from superstitious fears.

Now that people were becoming more objective in their assessments, there were few stories that had originated solely in the imagination or in cases of mistaken identity. Certainly there were tales of his activities still to be heard in rural gossip, but those that were proven and documented were of a rather special kind, as we shall see.

To close the chapter, then, I propose to look at his last three widely publicised exploits in the century. Then, in the next chapter, but still in the nineteenth century, I shall

---

* In *Stand & Deliver,* Elizabeth Villiers adds two more similar but undated instances to this list: "In Lambeth an old woman was found strangled in an upper room, the door locked, the window open, and of her murderer no trace remaining. Public opinion declared he was Spring Heeled Jack. What more plain, they said? Evidently he had leaped up from the garden to that open window on the second floor and so had entered to commit his crime. The story was not convincing, there was nothing to connect the mysterious being with it, but the search redoubled, and had Spring Heeled Jack been found he would have died upon the gallows. A young woman was also found dead on a lonely footpath. She had died of heart disease, but the rumour insisted she had seen Jack and been frightened to death by him — which is probable." It is a pity that Miss Villiers was not able to add more detail about the young girl in the light of her suggestion.

recount the remarkable story of the actual capture of a
Spring Heeled Jack, and a mysterious report from Devon
which some authorities believe may have been Spring Heeled
Jack's most spectacular achievement.

The first of these instances returns us to the scene of
one of Jack's very earliest forays, the district of Peckham,
from where, you will recall, an anonymous resident wrote
to the Lord Mayor of London to draw attention to the
leaping terror. It may have come as a surprise to Londoners
that Jack had returned to his old haunts — it certainly
was to the *News of the World* which reported the affair on
November 17 1872:

> Seeing the altered state of things in these days, it might have
> been thought that any successful revival of such a piece of folly
> or wickedness [as that of Spring Heeled Jack] was impossible.
> Our suburbs are not only lit, but watched, and in place of fields
> and lanes, consist, for the most part, of broad thoroughfares with
> dwellings in all directions.
>
> In spite of this South London is even now in a state of commo-
> tion owing to what is known as the Peckham Ghost. Not the stone
> throwing 'ghost' which a few months since destroyed scores of
> panes of glass in certain streets, but a mysterious figure, quite as
> alarming in manners and appearance as that which terrified a
> previous generation.
>
> As in all such cases much has been set down to popular exagger-
> ation, and the tendency of stories of the wild and wonderful to
> grow in the telling. This we can hardly be expected to credit,
> that the figure in question is eight feet in height, springs over
> stone walls and lofty hedges, and on nearing a victim changes
> suddenly from grim blackness to luminous white.

The paper then goes on to try and sort fact from fiction
in the reported instances.

The terror was first seen by a carrier as he was driving his
wagon in Lordship Lane. 'The figure suddenly darted out of
a field,' says the article, 'and the carrier was so terrified by
the suddeness of the thing that instead of applying his
horse-whip to good purpose — instead of leaving his mark on
the miscreant in an unmistakable manner — he lashed his
horse into a gallop.'

He was, though, more clearly seen by two young local girls — as always Jack's favourite target.

> On the evening of Sunday week, two of the daughters of Dr Carver, the headmaster of Dulwich College — young girls of from fourteen to sixteen years of age — were, with their governess, setting out for church. The younger of the two happened to be in advance, and had just passed through the open doorway on to the step, when she saw moving rapidly towards her across the carriage-drive, at about eight or ten yards distance, a figure with arms extended.
>
> Startled and alarmed, the young lady screamed out, and sprang hastily back into the porch, communicating her fright to her companions. They, meanwhile, had caught sight of the miscreant; but in the alarm and confusion which ensued — the door being only partly open — they were unable to observe in which direction he made his escape.

The following day, the newspaper says, a search of the grounds was made, and down-trodden grass was found behind a bush where someone had obviously stationed themself.

The terror made several more appearances in Peckham, but was obviously a pale imitation of his predecessor, as he never grappled with any of his victims and took to his heels at the first scream. But like the man from whom he had taken his *modus operandi*, he later faded from view uncaptured and unrepentant.

Another far bolder and daring Jack appeared in Lincolnshire in 1877 and was witnessed by virtually the entire population of the town of Caistor. The *Lincolnshire Times* relates the story in a Christmas issue:

> The strange being appeared in the neighbourhood of the town and created little short of panic by jumping on to the roof of a cottage and running over house-tops.
>
> Crowds soon assembled as news of the appearance got about, and the people watched him jump from the ground onto the roof of an old Roman building. Here he was fired at by a man with a gun.
>
> But with superhuman activity he bounded from one part of the town to another, some of his leaps being to the height of twenty

feet and more.

As he ran along the walls of the New Barracks, he was again fired at, but, as before, without any apparent effect. All attempts to corner him and prove if he were spirit or human being failed.

Summarising the incident, The *Lincolnshire Times* added, 'His approaches were always effected without the slightest noise, and all attempts to catch or hit him, either with bullets or stones failed. According to sketches made of him from the descriptions of eye witnesses, he had huge ears and was wearing a garment resembling a sheep skin with a peculiar tail.'

Now, mention of an army barracks leads us naturally into perhaps the most sensational of his later appearances. This also took place in 1877.

On a bright, moonlight night in the August of that year, Private John Regan was on sentry duty at Aldershot's North Camp. He had been detailed to the gates of the powder magazine and was standing at ease in his sentry box when he heard a harsh, grating sound.

Private Regan stiffened and pricked up his ears. It sounded very much as if someone was dragging a heavy metal object along the road. Had there been a break-in at the powder magazine and was someone trying to make off with a case of gunpowder? The thought raced through his head as he cocked his rifle and stepped out of his box.

He peered up and down the road which was fully illuminated by the moonlight, but there was nothing to be seen. He looked across at the other sentry box, thirty feet away at the far side of the gates, but there was no sign his colleage had heard anything untoward. He shrugged his shoulders and decided he must have been imagining things.

But as he stepped back into his sentry box again he felt what he later described as the touch of a hand 'icy and death-like' on his cheek.

He screamed with fright and almost dropped his rifle. The sound brought the sentry from the other box running to his side. And as the two men stood side by side in the moonlight, a huge figure leapt over their heads and landed without a sound on the road in front of them.

Rooted to the spot with fear, the two soldiers stared at the amazing sight before them. It seemed like a man in a tight-fitting oilskin-like suit wearing a shining helmet and grinning malevolently at them.

For a moment neither man moved, then with shaking fingers Regan raised his still cocked rifle and challenged the creature in an unsteady voice, 'Who goes there?'

There was absolute silence, after which the creature made a sudden bound foward. The startled Regan pressed the trigger and the bullet seemed to pass right through the being, he said later.

The figure took another step and then leapt high into the air. As he passed over the two soldiers he belched a stream of blue flame into their faces. Both fell back in panic, scrabbling with their rifles.

Leaping onto the top of Regan's sentry box, the creature paused once more and a hollow laugh rang around the camp. Both soldiers took aim at him but when their bullets seemed to have not the slightest effect, they turned on their heels and fled.

At first the story the two men told was ridiculed by their superiors, who charged them with deserting their posts and sentenced them to hard labour. But when the same figure appeared again — and again — there was no alternative but to believe them and set them free.

Although the Army did its best to discourage publicity about the incident, it was impossible to keep such a story quiet, and the more sensational papers like *The Illustrated Police News*, which made a speciality of describing and depicting the fantastic and the gruesome, had a field day with it. In its issue of September 8 1877 under a suitably dramatic picture (reproduced on facing page), the paper wrote,

> Not long ago speculation of every sort was at its height as to the so-called ghost, or as the soldiers irreverently styled him, 'Spring Heeled Jack.' Suspicion finally settled upon one particular corps, for the reason that the ghost had hitherto only been seen where this regiment was stationed. The corps in question, however, has now left Aldershot and the authorities were much astonished when they learnt that 'Spring Heeled Jack' had re-appeared.

Jack visualised as a ghost in this front page illustration from the Illustrated Police News *of September 8, 1877.*

His method of proceeding seems to be to approach unobserved some post, then climb the sentry box, and pass his hand which is arranged to feel as cold and clammy as that of a corpse over the face of the sentinel. The sentries had lately been ordered to fire on the ghost, and were loaded with ball, but this precaution has lately been given up.

The re-appearance of the 'ghost' has caused a great sensation, principally one of indignation, and the authorities are determined this time to exhaust every means towards discovering the culprit.

Unfortunately the 'exhaustive' efforts of the authorities proved insufficient to discourage Spring Heeled Jack until he had had enough of his pranks; nor could they discover who the culprit might be.

Much later a solution and a possible culprit was offered by a writer in *Notes & Queries* which seems to me to carry the weight of conviction. The 'detective' was a Mr Alfred C.E. Welby, and he wrote in the issue of June 22 1907:

> More than thirty years ago jumping pranks were played many nights on the sentry over the magazine by the canal near the Camp at Aldershot. It was a lonely spot at some distance from the guard room.
>
> Jack used to spring across the canal while the sentry, pacing his beat, was walking away from it, and then on to the man's shoulders, sorely frightening him, and usually disarming him by carrying off his rifle.
>
> The pranks were popularly attributed to a lively officer of Rifles; he certainly was not convicted of them, and I do not know that he ever acknowledged himself to be Spring Heeled Jack.

Whether this man might ever have admitted a part in building the legend of the leaping terror, we shall now certainly never know. But not long after this there was another person who took to playing the role of Spring Heeled Jack and was actually caught and brought to justice.

It is a remarkable story which we shall consider next. And all the more remarkable because he was unmasked by a group of schoolboys!

6

The Schoolboys who caught Spring Heeled Jack!

Harleigh Severne (1838-1895) is now one of that multitude of Victorian authors whose name means virtually nothing to modern readers and whose works are only to be found in the dustiest corners of second-hand bookshops. During his lifetime, however, he enjoyed a modest success, enabling him to live with reasonable comfort in Kidderminster, Worcestershire, where he was born and brought up.

He produced somewhere in the region of two dozen books during his lifetime, a mixture of novels and works of non-fiction, and was regarded by his London publishers, Griffith and Farren, as a reliable if unspectacular seller. Perhaps his best works were those for younger readers, and one particular title, *Little Harry Gwynne* (1874) went through several editions.

He was a man of quiet tastes who enjoyed walking in the picturesque countryside near his home, and made only rare excursions to nearby Birmingham and the much further distant London. He was steeped in local lore and traditions, and it comes as no surprise to find that his books are full of bits of information and tales about the Worcestershire countryside. In one of these is to be found the story of Harleigh Severne's encounter with Spring Heeled Jack.

The book is called *Chums: A Tale for the Youngsters* and

it was published in 1878 by Griffith and Farren. It enjoyed the distinction of eight line drawings by the popular Victorian illustrator, Harry Furniss, and was described by its author as 'a story of my childhood's days'.

It is, in fact, a record of Severne's own schooldays at a boarding school in Bewdley, a small town just over three miles from Kidderminster. It was here that he was sent at the age of seven by his father, a none-too-successful local businessman. He was an only child, his mother having died earlier and it became necessary for him to be boarded when the nurse who looked after him left to get married. The experiences which followed at the school formed the basis of the book.

As was almost traditional with Victorian writers, Severne partly disguised Bewdley as 'Brookford', called himself 'Bernard Ayres', and referred to his schoolfriends by their Christian names only. But as he admitted in a small auto-biographical article in the publishing trade magazine, *The Bookman,* in August 1878, 'the places and the boys were those I had known. . . and the story of 'Springall Jack' was true also, though the man's real name I forget.' For this reason I believe the tale is well worth retelling here.

The story begins with the problems the new boy experiences while settling in at Brookford. Gradually, however, he builds up a friendship with three other lads, all slightly older than himself, Harry, Mat and another who is nick-named 'Scamp'. In their company, young Bernard soon discovers there is more to school than work. One evening as the group are returning home at dusk from a walk in the countryside with the school dog 'Hero', Harry makes the most of the gathering gloom to tell them a story:

> 'You know that lonely part of the road that we're coming to,' (he says) 'between the top of this hill and the sweet shop, where we buy those whopping big bulls'-eyes? Well, it is somewhere there where "Springall Jack" frightens people so.'
>
> 'Let's keep up with the others,' I interposed, hurrying on.
>
> 'He scared Old Betsy half out of her skin,' continued Harry, his voice sinking into a low, awed whisper. 'You've heard about "Springall Jack" haven't you? Spring-*heeled* Jack' he used to be called at first, because he is supposed to wear boots with such

enormous springs in them that he can clear a six-foot wall at a single bound. So he goes about in the lonely parts of the country, scaring people awfully, by suddenly jumping over a gate or a hedge, right in their very faces, just when they are walking quietly along, never dreaming of anyone being near them, and before they can say "Jack Robinson", he has sprung over the opposite wall, and has disappeared from their sight, uttering a yell that makes their blood run cold. But now the name for him has got currupted into "Spring-all Jack", because its shorter, as well as more expressive, don't you see? Some people have shortened it still more by calling him "Springle Jack"; you'll hear all the boys speak of him so, down in Brookford, but I like to see it spelt "Spring*all*" best, even if you do pronounce it like "Springle" as most people do. Sometimes he lies by a heap of stones, till his victims come close up to him; then he jumps up suddenly, slings up his arms, and, with an unearthly shout, springs past them, and disappears over the wall, or hedge. He has half killed some people from sheer fright, and the bobbies are after him, to try and catch him. Only they don't know who he is at all, and he don't give them much chance to find out either!'

The boys are naturally a little frightened at Harry's story, but he goes on to try and reassure them.

'Oh, you needn't be scared; he's safe not to be in the same place again tonight. It wouldn't pay, don't you see? He would be caught, sure enough, if he tried that on. But, you see, he watches for people who are certain to be dreadfully frightened, and who can't do anything. If he saw, or heard, the peelers coming, he'd be off like a shot, and they would never see him at all.'

By now darkness has almost completely fallen, and despite their show of bravado, the boys are all somewhat uneasy. Their senses are alert to any sound and they even link arms to gain confidence from proximity to each other. Little Bernard begins to sniffle a bit and admits, in hindsight, 'Even now, when I walk through country lanes on a dark night, the recollection of the taste of those salt tears rises forcibly to my mind, and over the leafy hedgerows, I conjure up the hiding forms and peering faces which every waving bough seemed to shadow forth to my heated, childish fancy on that eventful night.'

They reach the top of the hill and press on between the high stone walls, Harry had mentioned in his story. Suddenly, the dog 'Hero' lets out a low growl and bounds off ahead into the darkness. The boys, now really afraid, stop and huddle against the wall. There is another short bark from 'Hero' and then —

> 'A sudden whizzing past us, as of flying garments, and we were conscious — all of us but Harry, who, with a silent shudder through his whole frame, had buried his face on Scamp's shoulder — that a huge, shapeless form had risen above the level of the wall, almost grazing us as we cowered down before it, and, standing out for a moment in black relief against the leaden sky, had sunk slowly down again upon the other side.

> 'Before we had time to draw a gasping breath of relief, another sound rivetted our attention. It was the quick scrabbling of feet upon the stones, and the next moment a long, lithe body rose above our heads, and dropped down upon the other side as quickly as the first had done.

> 'It's "Hero",' whispered Mat, under his breath. "Hero" was growling, fiercely, loudly — breaking forth now and again into a pained, angry bark, as the dull thud of a stick, and the deep tones of a man's voice, fell upon our ears, telling us plainly that, amongst a volley of oaths, our faithful old dog was defending us from harm, perhaps at the peril of his very life.'

The boys grab this opportunity to take to their heels and dash up the lane — running full tilt into a teacher, Mrs Royce, and the school gardener who have been sent out to find where they are. As they gasp out their story that they have seen 'Springall Jack', the dog runs up with a fragment of dark grey cloth in his mouth. Both the teacher and the gardener agree it must have been torn from the cloak of the leaping terror.

Despite the fright of this evening, it does not dampen the boys' high spirits and a few weeks later Scamp suggests that Harry and Bernard go on another 'spree' with him. He refuses to say just what he has in mind, or why they are to go, but they are to 'spy' on a man named Rylands who keeps a number of donkeys in a ramshackle stable not far from the school.

Reluctantly, Bernard allows himself to be talked into going, and later that day finds himself squashed down with the other two behind a hedge at the back of the stable waiting for Rylands to appear. It is Scamp who whispers them to silence as he hears footsteps approaching.

'It was Rylands who entered; the "Lanky Man" as we used always to call him — an unusually tall and thin man "all arms and legs" as the Scamp used often to say. He was apparently middle-aged, though possibly his grizzly grey hair and deep-set eyes may have made him look older than he really was; his hollow cheeks, too, were grimy with coal dust, for amongst the variety of uses to which his ill-kept, hardly-used animals were put, was that of dragging heavy cartloads of coal from door to door, amongst the villages scattered around.

The 'Lanky Man' Rylands trying out his spring-heeled boots.
An illustration by Harry Furniss for the novel Chums.

'The half-starved donkeys instinctively shrunk away from him as they saw him enter, turning their meek, suffering-looking eyes upon him, as though they would have besought him to spare them, for once, the torture of the customary dig-in-the-ribs from the short, sharp stick he carried, with which he usually saluted them as he passed.

'Just now, however, he seemed to be intent upon some other sport than that of brutally worrying his hapless dependents, and, with a half-muttered oath, he strode on, until he came so close to where I was sitting, watching, in a state of nervous agitation lest we should be discovered, that I expect I should have heedlessly proclaimed our presence by a sudden cry of alarm, had not my very fear almost restrained the use of my faculties.

'It was so strange, so weird! The gloom of the building, the forbidding, scaring aspect of the man, and his coarse behaviour, as well as the bitter knowledge that we were doing wrong in thus being "out of bounds" at all, and trespassers too, moreover, all combined to work me up to the highest pitch of fear and excitement.

'Still I watched on at my hole, never daring to move a muscle, though my limbs were aching all over from the strain of preserving for so long a time, the same position.

'Rylands at once proceeded to pull away a portion of a stack of fagots, piled unsuspiciously against the opposite side of the shed, leaving exposed, as he did so, a large square board, to which was attached, by way of a handle, a long loop of stout iron wire.

'Stooping down, he lifted this away, and from the cavity beneath, pulled forth some long, black objects, not very easily distinguishable in this dim light.

'A faint perception of Scamp's mysterious design in bringing us to this odd place, now gradually dawned across my brain, making me shudder with an agony of dread, as the light broke slowly in upon my mind.

'A sudden, irresistible cry rose to my lips, but happily died away again, before its utterance had hurled us abruptly into an unknown, terrible danger. A desire to cry, rather than an actual sound; a gasping, catching breath, such as wakes one sometimes, startled and afraid — one knows not why — from a restless, disturbed slumber.

'Only how could Scamp have had any clue to this solution of the dreaded mystery?

'But this was no place for questioning him, and in the meantime, I could scarcely feel more shocked and bewildered, by any fresh revelations, than I did at that moment, when I instinctively knew myself to be for the second time in the awful presence of "Springall Jack."

'Yes! there are his boots! for now he is pulling them on, muttering to himself the while; and in another minute he will be upon his feet once more, equipped in those instruments of such terrible torture to the nervous and the weak.

'A horrid thought flashed through my brain.

'What if he were intending to practise leaping the very hedge under which we were seated?

'But no. He would scarcely dare to hazard an experiment so dangerous to his own safety, in broad daylight, even in so unfrequented, out-of-the-way a spot as this lonely by-lane.

'He had risen to his feet now, towering there to much over six feet, in those high, spring-heeled boots of his.

'Then, with a sudden bound, he sprang high into the air, descending close to the two terrified donkeys who, with a sprightlier movement than before, rushed helter-skelter to the spot which their master had just vacated.

'But ere they were half way across, he had turned, and, with marvellous agility, was once more springing through the air, this time right over the backs of the affrighted animals, who, in their bewilderment, now stood stock still close together, their heads touching, and their noses close upon the ground.

'With a hoarse, chuckling kind of laugh, he continued his exertions for two or three more flights, until, apparently, satisfied with his practice, he slowly removed his boots, and placed them once more in concealment, covering everything up as before.

'Then he rushed upon the awe-struck donkeys, hitched them in a trice into one of the rickety carts, and opening the doors wide, belaboured them unmercifully as he drove them across the field to the cottage.

'When the "click" of the gate reached us, as it swung back after they had all passed through — and not until then — we breathed freely once more, as we looked at each other in unbroken silence.'

When they are at last sure that Rylands has gone, the three boys quickly leave their hiding place and hurry back to school. They both press Scamp to tell them how he found out that the donkey man was the local Spring Heeled Jack. Finally, he relieves their suspense:

'It was only from something funny that the "Lanky Man" said to me this morning, that I began to suspect. I was coming home from the village, after sending that telegram off for Mrs

Royce you know; and he stopped me, and asked me a lot of questions about our having seen Springall Jack the other night. I thought it was rather queer to ask so much about it now, because he has seen us lots of times since, and never said anything about it; and I told him so, too. Then he said the news had only reached him a day or two ago, and he hadn't seen any of us passing since, unless in the company of one of the teachers. I said it was odd that he should have heard it so long after, seeing he lived so near to us, for I had been told that it was all over the village the very next day.

'Well, I told him, then, that I was one of the very four who had seen Springall Jack, and he gave such a tremendous jump, when I said that, that I looked up at him quite surprised. And it was just that very moment that put me on the scent, for, as I looked up, it flashed through my mind all of a sudden, so that I began to call out something that I might have been sorry for afterwards.

'Fortunately, I didn't get very far before I remembered, and checked myself just in time. But for all that, I think he must have had some faint suspicion, for almost directly he told me that he had just come out of that shed, where he had been trying to see whether he could jump at all, and he didn't believe he could get over two feet, even if it were to save his life.'

Scamp expresses amazement to the others that Rylands should have given himself away so easily, and also surprise that they should have caught him red-handed the first time they had gone to watch at the stables. But they are now confronted by another dilemma — whether to expose the "Lanky Man" or not: for as they tell each other, to admit having seen him in the stables would mean admitting to having broken bounds without leave.

For several days, the boys are tortured with doubts about whether they should reveal their secret to the teachers or the police. But the thought of punishment for disobeying the rules keeps them quiet.

Then fate intervenes when they are out for a coach ride and they overhear their driver mention the name 'Springall Jack':

' "So they've caught him at last, have they?" I heard our driver say; for, as he leaned over to speak to his friend, I could overhear, distinctly, every word he uttered.

' "Yes, that they have. Three of them — peelers, you know, —

dressed up as old women, and then, when he showed himself, of course, they pretended to be awfully frightened, and ran off in different directions. He chivied one of them, and the other two, dodging round, got behind him and collared him, unawares like."

"Ah! That was a neat little job!"

' "Ay, you're right there! But they had a fine hard struggle to secure him, I can tell you. Even with the three of them, he nearly got off, they say; he was so tall, and wiry, and so desperate like; then their women's clothes hampered them, not being used to manage petticoats and shawls, don't you see? One of them had to draw his truncheon at last, or "Springall Jack" wouldn't have been in private lodgings at the town's expense *this* night, I reckon!"

' "Ha! ha! You don't say so? Well, and who has it turned out to be, now that they *have* secured him?"

' "Eh, that's the rub! and more than I can tell you. Why, they haven't gone into the police station, not scarcely ten minutes ago, and being in the dark, you see, and everything done so completely on the quiet like, there isn't any one but the officials as has the least idea who it *can* be, and *they* are all just as mum, as, — as, — that there town pump as won't fetch up the water except by fits and starts, just as it pleases like. And it isn't for no want of trying to pump it out of 'em, neither, for the news spread just like wild fire, and there's a many of the folks as 'ud give their very tongues, a'most, to know the name — only that then they'd lose the pleasure of telling of it. Did you *ever* see the town in such a state of inside-out like?"

' "No, that I haven't, not since Lord Brookford came of age, that I can remember; and that's many a long year back, now. Why, there's folks out at every door, and groups under each lamp-post, all the way down the street as we came along."

' "What are you stopping so long for, coachman?" inquired Mrs Royce, impatiently, from the far end of the seat, while I and the boys just round the speakers were listening breathlessly to the recital.

' "They have just caught "Springle Jack", ma'am!" answered the driver briefly, and turning round with a "See you again presently!" to his informant, he started his horses off at a brisk pace towards home.

'A shudder ran through my frame at his words, wrought upon as my nerves were by the exciting conversation I had overheard.'

Bernard and his three friends then suffer a night of anxiety wondering what will happen next. Their question is answered the following morning when they are summoned before Mrs

Royce. She tells them that a policeman has already been up to the school and, knowing that they had seen 'Springall Jack' on one of his nocturnal jaunts, they were to be asked to give evidence at the man's trial. With sinking hearts they realise they have no alternative.

Later in the morning all four are taken to the local Magistrate's Court, which is packed with people anxious to see who the agile terror might be. When Rylands is brought into the dock a wave of amazed conversation breaks over the room.

Bernard, however, is kept outside while his friends give evidence, and when he is finally taken into the courtroom, the lawyer defending Rylands, a Mr Green, immediately protests about yet another young witness. He insists that while his client does not deny he was caught wearing boots with springs in the heels the previous evening, that was the only occasion when he had performed such a practical joke. He was certainly not the 'Springall Jack' who had been terrifying the neighbourhood during recent weeks.

When the lawyer is then pressed by the Magistrate to answer where his client had got the boots from, he replies that they were lent to him 'by the veritable "Springall Jack" whose name he is, in honour bound, unable to betray'.

Mr Green maintains that he will show 'not only that the witnesses are mistaken as to the prisoner's identity with the person seen upon all former occasions, but that his (the prisoner's) whereabouts, on each night in question, can be easily accounted for.' Despite this plea, he is told to continue examining the witnesses.

The lawyer therefore addresses Bernard who has been put in the witness box:

> 'It was quite dark when you saw this strange being, I think. Too dark to see whether the figure was tall or short, or stout, or thin, or anything — wasn't it?
>
> 'It was tall and thin,' I said, 'I saw it plain enough against the sky, when it jumped over the wall. It was the Lanky Man. I am *sure*. I didn't know it at the time, but I knew him again the moment I saw him the second time.
>
> 'I pulled up short. "The second time!" What had possessed me? Somehow, I had forgotten the people around, and even the presence

of the dreaded man himself, in my earnest protest as to his identity. And now this sudden unaccountable impulse had doubtless placed me in the dreadful position of a forced betrayer of that secret adventure, which we had pledged ourselves not to divulge to anyone.

'The titters of the audience — I suppose at my unconscious use of our schoolboy nickname — and the angry stamp of the prisoner, recalled me suddenly to myself — alas! only too late.

' "The second time?" repeated the chairman, catching at my words; "when was that?" '

Bernard looks unavailingly down at his friends and realises he has given the game away. When questioned further he admits that he promised not to say anything about the stable incident because of the boys' fear of being punished for breaking the school rules. Who did he make the promise to? Bernard breaks into tears and can only point silently at Scamp.

When Scamp is placed in the witness box again, he is asked by the Magistrate to confirm the second encounter with Rylands and whether it was definitely him the boys saw.

'I should rather think it was,' he replied, 'Why it was broad day-light, don't you know? — at least it was in the evening — and we saw him go into his shed and watched him take those boots out of a hiding-place and then begin to jump about right over those donkeys of his and I expect that's where he keeps the cloak and if you like I could show any one the very spot.'

'There was an excited murmur of astonishment all over the room as he went running on, regardless of stops, rising to such a pitch as the interest increased, that the police had to threaten to turn out sundry offenders, who paid no heed to their continued cries of "Hush! hush!" or "Silence, there!"

'A fierce, angry stamp, from those restless feet in the dock, indicated, plainly enough, the rage and annoyance of the prisoner, at this fresh and most conclusive phase in the evidence.

'And so, little by little, with a question here and a suggestion there, the lawyers engaged upon the case contrived to worm out from the Scamp the whole story of our disobedience on that adventurous night, until, when the recital ended, Mr Green's case seemed to have grown as hopeless and desperate as it was possible for it to be.'

The evidence of the boys is indeed enough to commit Rylands to trial at the next Assizes and his application for bail is refused, much to the relief of all those present. When the youngsters leave the court building they find themselves the 'heroes of the day' for having brought 'Springall Jack' to justice. And although later they are reproved by their teacher for having broken bounds, are let off any punishment because of the special circumstances involved.

The story of 'Springall Jack' does not arise again in *Chums* until nearly the end of the book when the trial of Rylands is referred to. As Bernard himself is ill in bed at the time, he is not called upon to give evidence, but the others who do attend return later to the school with a voluble description of the proceedings at Rockenham Winter Assizes.

And it is only appropriate that the boy who first realised who 'Springall Jack' was should fill in the final details of the episode:

> "He has got in for it pretty stiffly, too, poor wretch!" said the Scamp. "Three years' hard labour, and five years' police surveillance". And he made a wry face, as he slurred over the pronunciation of the last word of the verdict, which he had learnt by heart.

Today *Chums* is a forgotten book, and probably deservedly so, for beyond the 'Springall Jack' episode the remainder of the story is rather insipid and full of heavy moralising. Yet the encounter of the small boys with the agile terror is well drawn and all the more interesting because, as I have said, it is based on fact.

To confirm this I decided to check in Worcester to see if I could fill in the final details and locate the actual case in which Severne was involved and the real name of the man concerned. It proved a relatively simple matter for, as Severne was born in 1838 and was seven at the time of the incident, the year 1845 was obviously the crucial one. And sure enough documented in the records of the Worcester Assizes for November 1845 was the information that Thomas Rowland, carrier, of Bewdley, Kidderminster, was sentenced to three years hard labour and five years police surveillance for committing a breach of public order. . . namely the impersonating of 'Springall Jack' to the disturbance of the populace.

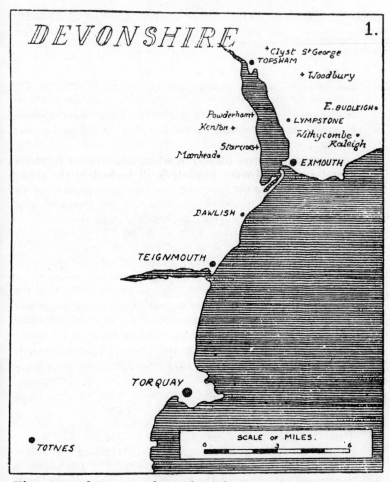

The area of Devon where the 'Phantom Footprints in the Snow' were reported in February 1855.

Perhaps the most extraordinary event which has been ascribed to the activities of Spring Heeled Jack is the case of the 'Devil's Hoofmarks' which occurred in Devon in February 1855. This story arose from the discovery on a snowy morning of a row of footmarks which extended across a large area of the countryside and had seemingly been made by someone — or something — capable of prodigeous agility.

The Times broke the news to the world in a story headlined 'Extraordinary Occurrence' in its issue of February 16:

> Considerable sensation has been evoked in the towns of Topsham, Lympstone, Exmouth, Teignmouth and Dawlish, in the south of Devon, in consequence of the discovery of a vast number of foot-tracks of a most strange and mysterious description. The superstitious go so far as to believe that they are the marks of Satan himself; and that great excitement has been produced among all classes may be judged from the fact that the subject has been descanted on from the pulpit.

> It appears that on Thursday night last (February 8) there was a very heavy fall of snow in the neighbourhood of Exeter and the south of Devon. On the following morning, the inhabitants of the above towns were surprised at discovering the tracks of some strange and mysterious creature, endowed with the powers of ubiquity, as the foot-prints were to be seen in all kinds of inaccessible places — on the tops of houses and narrow walls, in gardens and courtyards enclosed by high walls and palings, as well as in open fields. There was hardly a garden in Lympstone where the foot-prints were not observed.

> The track appeared more like that of a biped than a quadruped, and the steps were generally eight inches in advance of each other. The impressions of the feet closely resembled that of a donkey's shoe, and measured from an inch and a half to (in some instances) two and a half inches across. Here and there it appeared to be cloven, but in the generality of the steps the shoe was continuous, and from the snow in the centre remaining entire, merely showing the outer crest of the foot, it must have been convex.

> The creature seems to have approached the doors of several houses and then to have retreated, but no one has been able to discover the standing or resting point of this mysterious visitor. On Sunday last the Rev. Mr. Musgrave alluded to the subject in his sermon, and suggested the possibility of the footprints being those of a kangaroo; but this could scarcely have been the case, as they were found on both sides of the estuary of the Exe.

> At present it remains a mystery, and many superstitious people in the above towns are actually afraid to go outside their doors at night.

As the footprints were literally under the noses of the entire population across an area of 35 miles or so, they were as much a matter for examination as well as speculation. There were those who sought the logical explanation that they must have been made by an animal of some kind:

but what kind of animal could cover such an area during the few hours of darkness? The superstitious plumped for the Devil himself: but why should he have failed to single anyone out for a visitation? Lastly, a third school of thought wondered if that leaping terror, Spring Heeled Jack, had passed their way in the night?

In any event, while the locals debated the matter with a certain wariness, the correspondence columns of the national papers were soon resounding to all manner of theories from a host of brash would-be 'experts'. Their conclusions, hotly defended despite frequent crushing derision, ranged through a variety of birds and animals including swans, cranes, bustards, waders, and otters, rats, hares, polecats, frogs, badgers and, of course, the previously mentioned kangaroo.

It took a more rational correspondent of *The Times* who signed himself 'South Devon' and was clearly a local man, to get the matter in perspective:

This mysterious visitor (he wrote) generally only passed *once* down or across each garden or courtyard, and did so in nearly all the houses in many parts of the several towns mentioned, as also in the farms scattered about; this regular track passing in some instances over the roofs of houses, and hayricks, and very high walls (one 14 feet), without displacing the snow on either side or altering the distance between the feet, and passing on as if the wall had not been any impediment. The gardens with high fences or walls, and gates locked, were equally visited as those open and unprotected.

Now when we consider the distance that must have been gone over to have left these marks — I may say in almost every garden, on door-steps, through extensive woods of Luscombe, upon commons, in enclosures and farms — the actual progress must have exceeded a hundred miles. It is very easy for people to laugh at these appearances and account for them in an idle way. At present no satisfactory solution has been given. No known animal could have traversed this extent of country in one night, besides having to cross an estuary of the sea two miles broad. Neither does any known animal walk in a *line* of single foot-steps, not even man.

Birds could not have left these marks, as no bird's foot leaves the impression of a hoof, or, even were there a bird capable of doing so, could it proceed in the direct manner above stated — nor would birds, even had they donkey's feet, confine themselves to one direct line, but hop here and there; but the nature

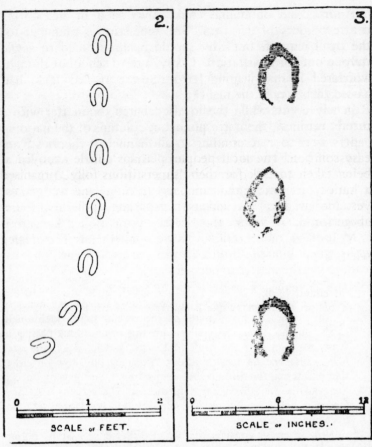

Close-up of the mysterious foot-marks. (Left) A sketch made by the eye-witness 'South Devon' and (right) a similar one drawn by 'G.M.M.' Both were published in The Times.

of the mark at once sets aside its being the track of a bird.

Besides, the most singular circumstances connected with it was that this particular mark removed the snow, wherever it appeared, clear, as if cut with a diamond, or branded with a hot iron; of course, I am not alluding to its appearance after having been trampled upon, or meddled with by the curious in and around the thoroughfares of the towns. In one instance this track entered a covered shed, and passed through it out of a broken part of the wall at the other end, where the atmosphere could not effect it.

Another correspondent, 'G.M.M.', who said he 'lived in the centre of the district where the alarm was first given', took the trouble to sketch a line of the tracks which *The Times* duly reproduced (also reprinted here). He added, 'I have addressed communications to the British Museum, to the Zoological Society, to the keepers of birds and beasts in the Regent's Park menagerie, and the universal reply is, they are utterly unable to form any conjecture on the subject.'

It was clear to everyone by now that there would be no easy solution. The local people, perhaps a little annoyed at being taken to task for their 'superstitious folly', organised a hunt to follow the course of the tracks — and were in for yet another surprise, which they subsequently kept quiet about for fear of yet more ridicule.

Years later, in December 1889, a Mr R. H. Busk revealed what happened on this 'expedition' in *Notes & Queries:*

> 'The track was followed up by hounds and huntsmen and crowds of country folk, till at last, in a wood (I think it was said over Dawlish) the hounds came back baying and terrified. This was the moment when one would think the real excitement would begin. Nevertheless no one seems to have had the courage to rush in where the dogs feared to tread, and the matter ended in a battle of conjecture. The most general local impression seems to have been that it was the devil put his foot in it, though so widespread a belief in so useless and partial a manifestation of a personal devil seems incredible.'

Getting no satisfaction from the suggestions that neither beasts, birds or the devil were responsible for the tracks, some Devonians turned to Spring Heeled Jack whose widespread activities throughout Southern England were known to them, though he had rarely made excursions into their territory. Perhaps, ventured some, this was his *pièce de resistance?* A spectacular show of his fleet-footed abilities across a huge sweep of rural countryside — the snow carrying the imprint of his prowess for all to see.

Notes & Queries again carries the most relevant information. In the March 1 1890 issue a Mr W. Courthope Forman said he had been a child of seven living in South Devon at the time and the footprints had made a deep and lasting impression upon him:

'My most vivid recollection of the matter is in connexion with the home of friends living at Exmouth. Here, the footprints came up the front garden to within a few feet of the house, stopped abruptly, and began again in the garden at the back within a few feet of the building ... just as if the demon had made a gigantic leap.'

All the hallmarks of a Spring Heeled Jack 'prank' some might venture to suggest?

With the passage of time, both the animal and bird theories have been dismissed by experts for there is not a single known creature that fits all the requirements of the tracks. And the 'demon' suggestion has little to commend it, although interestingly it was proposed in the last word on the matter at the time which appeared in the form of a letter to the *Illustrated London News* of March 17 1855. Writing from Heidelberg in Germany, a reader signing himself 'C.C.C.' said,

'I beg the favour of you to insert in your newspaper the following fact, upon the authority of a Polish Doctor in Medicine living in the neighbourhood: — On the Piashowa-gora, a small hill on the borders of Gallacia, but in Russian Poland, every year are to be seen in the snow the same foot-prints as those seen in Devonshire, in a single line round the hill, at a few inches and regular distance from each other; no mark of a beginning or end being distinguished. It is universally attributed by the inhabitants to supernatural influence.'

So do I believe one of the impersonators of Spring Heeled Jack was responsible for this mysterious event? The devil I do!*

---

* In *Notes & Queries*, March 16, 1907, it is stated that a story *The Flying Man* from the book *The Revelations of Inspector Morgan* by Oswald Crawfurd (1906) was based on the idea of Spring Heeled Jack being responsible for the 'Phantom Footprints in the Snow' and the reader is recommended to this fascinating work which is an early collection of detective stories all based on the cases of a Scotland Yard Inspector.

7

The Terror of Entertainment

It will come as no surprise to the reader to learn that after all this activity and the subsequent notoriety, Spring Heeled Jack soon developed into a popular character for the mediums of entertainment. A figure that had so quickly become a legend was heaven-sent for authors, playwrights, theatre managers and, in the fullness of time, magazine and comic publishers, film-makers and even advertisers.

By the later part of the nineteenth century he was an established by-word in the English language. His name was already being employed to describe anyone of agility, while his fearsome appearance was in common usage by many nurses and nannies to quieten troublesome children.

He was, as we have already seen, a familiar figure in the newspapers, and hundreds of column inches detailing his activities — both real and supposed — are to be found in the press from the year 1838 onwards. He became as well-known to readers of 'The Thunderer' (*The Times*) as to buyers of the sensational penny papers, although they each had their own particular angle on his exploits. That he was good 'copy' was never in doubt — it was just a matter of whether the editor and his reporters deplored his unsavoury behaviour or had a sneaking regard for the way he out-witted the authorities and flouted the law.

It is believed there were several folk songs about his exploits, but none of the words — or information about

111

them — has survived as far as I have been able to establish. He was certainly featured in a number of the 'penny ballads' sold by street vendors, but again none of these extremely ephemeral items have escaped the ravages of time in any major collection.

He was, though, eagerly embraced by the small theatres and 'gaffs' of the 1840's onwards and here we are more fortunate with information.

The places of live entertainment in nineteenth century Britain were one of the few sources of pleasure open to the mass of the people. Though they had little money for the luxuries enjoyed by the wealthy, what they did have was gladly laid out for the excitement of a 'night at the play'.

In his splendid evocation of this era, *Victorian Melodramas* (1976), Professor James L. Smith has exactly caught the ambiance of these cheap theatres to which Mr and Mrs London flooded each night with their families and friends:

> 'They surged into the theatre at six o'clock, fortified themselves at intervals with huge ham sandwiches, pigs' trotters, fried soles, chipped potatoes, cans of porter and flat stone bottles filled with beer, and then stayed on till after midnight, sometimes rapt in wonder, sometimes bursting into song, exchanging salvoes with friends across the auditorium, quarrelling and fighting, cheering, hissing, clapping, booing, stamping and stinking to the very rafters. This was the truly popular audience such theatres had to please.'

The big cities were full of such theatres. London boasted dozens like the Britannia Saloon in Hoxton, the Pavilion in Whitechapel, the Royal Standard in Shoreditch, and the famous Victoria, which because of the many vivid dramas it staged became popularly known as "the bleedin' Vic"!

Inferior still to these places were the 'penny gaffs', usually improvised from run-down or derelict business premises, where freewheeling and unscrupulous entrepreneurs put on all manner of entertainments. The audiences were the very poorest and the actors at the ends of their careers through age or drink. The atmosphere was one of vice and corruption and according to social commentators like Henry Mayhew they were particularly adept at presenting " 'orrible murder".

Melodrama was indeed the staple diet of all these places — scorned as it was by the legitimate theatre. And what melodrama it was, portraying life in the sharpest divisions of black and white, with virtuous heroines and the most died-in-the-wool villains, and virtue always triumphant in the constant battle of good with evil. In a nutshell, they dramatised Mr and Mrs London's problems and provided them with perfect answers. As James L. Smith has also remarked on the importance of melodrama:

'It's violent extremes of emotional distress and physical disaster, its threats of instant death by poison, buzz-saw, rope or steel or railway track, its hostile universe or earthquake, ice-flows, avalanche and mill-race, its terrifying bandits, pirates, gypsies, tyrants, vampires, werewolves, gliding ghosts and flying Dutchmen, its prisons, gallows, chains and racks and wheels, its gloating villains, tortured heroes and defenceless heroines are all no more than a thrilling prelude to the ultimate defeat of guilt and a final tableau of triumphant innocence.'

Because of their great popularity, these theatres were constantly in need of fresh material; as Richard D. Altick has pointed out in *Victorian Studies in Scarlet* (1970): 'Nineteenth century melodrama was as voracious a consumer of scripts as is modern television, and no subject was drawn on more heavily by playwrights with impatient managers at their door than the incomparably dependable one of murder.'

Indeed crime in general was ideal fodder, the more up-to-date the better, and where more natural to look for this than the newspapers? So when Spring Heeled Jack impinged himself so dramatically onto the public consciousness, he was a natural contender for a place in such company.

We shall almost certainly never know where the leaping terror of London first made his appearance in a play, though a shrewd guess would be in one of the London 'penny gaffs' whose players could devise a drama around a current topic and have it in production within a matter of days.

Spring Heeled Jack was a near ideal subject for such drama, for the character of the villain was always portrayed as a cloaked figure with shiny boots and huge whiskers. Jack in real life already had two of these attributes, and a mask with flaming eyes was an even more villainous appendage than a moustache.

In his first stage appearances, Jack probably did no more than leap upon a series of female victims, evading the bumbling figures of the authorities (much to the delight of the audiences, no doubt) and leaving the audience with his laughter ringing in their ears. A 'penny gaff' play needed no real story, save a figure they could recognise, scarcely a beginning or an end, and merely some dramatic incidents at which the audience could alternately cheer and hiss.

The first proper play as such was probably 'Spring Heeled Jack, The Terror of London' written by John Thomas Haines in 1840. Haines wrote dozens of melodramas for the small London theatres and was particularly adept at utilising current topics.

As well as being a playwright, Haines had been an actor and even played in one or two of his own productions from time to time. In his later years, though, he was employed as stage manager at the English Opera House and could boast an intimate knowledge of all aspects of theatre life, both behind the scenes and on the boards. It was only the lack of copyright protection for his work which prevented him becoming a wealthy man as a result of his popularity as a dramatist.

In his version of the Spring Heeled Jack story, Haines dramatised the exploits of the mystery man who terrorised London as they had been reported in the press. However, true to the tradition of right triumphing over evil, he had the terror unmasked in the final scene as a blackguard who had been jilted by his sweetheart because of his unsavoury ways and consequently vowed vengeance on all women. It was only appropriate, of course, that the fair heroine on whom Jack had inflicted his most dastardly attacks should be responsible for getting him to expose himself by the use of flattery!

It was hardly a very original concept, but the play delighted audiences and was an enormous success mainly because of the clever use of scenery and special effects. By the 1840's

A film company poster for The Curse of the Wraydons *(1946), which was based on the earlier stage plays about* Spring Heeled Jack.

115

theatres were well equipped to heighten drama and the use of a diorama — a backcloth painted on long strips of canvas wound between vertical rollers — plus a 'flying rope', enabled the actor portraying Jack to make enormous leaps against a constantly changing terrain. There were also trap doors through which he could loom menacingly, and blood sachets hidden on the other actors which he could burst when he attacked them.

The success of this version lead, invariably, to it being plagiarized by other small theatres and the 'penny gaffs'. The story was also taken up by the owners of the small portable theatres, or 'peep shows', who carried their equipment from town to town charging a small coin for goggle-eyed viewers to watch tiny cardboard figures staged in various dramatic scenes. It was almost certainly being put on in some form by the troupes of touring actors who appeared at rural fairs across the country and whose rustic audiences needed none of the sophisticated trickery of the metropolitan theatres to believe what was put before them.

Perhaps the most successful of the Spring Heeled Jack plays was that staged at the Lyceum Theatre in London, which is still famous to this day, in particular because of its association with the great actor, Henry Irving, who appeared there from 1878 to 1902.

The play was revived in the 1870's by W.G. Wills, the eccentric portrait painter and resident dramatist at the Lyceum. He was the man responsible for some of Irving's best productions while the actor was building his reputation (*Charles I, Eugene Aram* and *Vanderdickan*), but also wrote a great deal of inferior work of which it is surprising to find *Spring Heeled Jack* classified although it enjoyed considerable success.

Wills' story was a much modified version of the earlier plays, and we shall be discussing it more fully later for it served as the basis of a film about Spring Heeled Jack called *The Curse of the Wraydons* (1946). I should perhaps mention that Jack's entrance was in the best traditions of the theatre, bounding in from the side on a 'flying rope'. Unfortunately, it is reported, this rope failed to work correctly on a number

of occasions and left the unfortunate actor suspended above
the stage while frantic scene shifters tried to lower him. Not
a predicament that the real Jack would have allowed himself to get into!

Sadly, as the century drew to its close, the theatre as
a whole was on the decline, and in place of the melodramas,
came the Music Halls, and after them the magic of films.
But Spring Heeled Jack was already a popular figure in
another medium, the 'Penny Dreadfuls'.

I have already discussed at length in a previous book,

*Spring Heeled Jack about to rescue Daisy Leigh from the
clutches of another blackguard! She was the heroine who
enjoyed his protection in the serial written by George
Augustus Sala.*

The Penny Dreadful (Gollancz, 1975) the history of these remarkable publications which entertained and thrilled generations of Victorians, young and old, but are now the rarest of rare collector's items. They were basically eight-page serials, published weekly at one penny, and featured stories about every area of human interest from romance to adventure, horror to the supernatural, pirates and high-waymen, and, of course, crime and murder.

They were published by a group of colourful and unscrupulous men based in the Fleet Street area who plagiarized the living and the dead, the famous and the not-so-famous, and most of all each other, with carefree abandon. They employed armies of wretched hacks to grind out these serials, week by week, paying them the barest minimum, and insisting on the maximum of drama in each part.

The niceties of publishing, as we now understand them, were thrown to the winds. Each part had a lurid illustration − or 'fierce' plate as they were called − on the first page, which might or might not have anything to do with the story. It could be a stock illustration if the publisher was short of money, or a specially commissioned item inserted in the hope of bolstering sales. There were never title pages and rarely even chapters. The stories were set in the smallest type and jammed into double columns on each page − finishing on the eighth page in mid-sentence, perhaps, and then continued in the next issue with the following word, without any attempt to tell the reader what had gone before! It was assumed he had been following the story; if not − and there were plenty of illiterates who bought the serials simply for the pictures and stumbled laboriously over the words − it was just too bad.

The unfortunate writers played fast and loose with their readers, too. If short on inspiration, they might well insert a totally extraneous short story they had standing by to fill up space, and as long as the serial was selling the publisher apparently could not have cared less. But if the public lost interest, the remedy was invariably drastic − the writer would be told to liven-up the story still more, and if this failed, he would be instructed to conclude it in the next issue, regardless of how a most complex set of characters

118

and situations would have to be resolved in a few paragraphs.

Despite these limitations, there is no denying the enormous popularity of these publications, and when Charles Knight, the renowned Victorian printer remarked that 'the penny magazine produced a revolution in popular art throughout the world' he hit the nail squarely on the head. By the 1840's, rudimentary education had been introduced so that people could read and write; the steam printing press had been invented and quick and inexpensive magazine production was now possible. What's more, the new means of transport by road and rail made possible the swift distribution of publications to catch any new public fancy.

As in the theatre, the 'Penny Dreadfuls' exemplified the struggle between good and evil, and offered the reader a similar kind of 'escape' from the trials of his drab everyday life. Like the stage, too, the publications drew heavily on well-known characters and subjects of immediate interest.

Spring Heeled Jack made his first appearance in this form in the eighteen forties — again I am afraid it has been impossible to establish the exact date. The best information I can lay my hands on is a note in *Notes and Queries* for May 18 1907, in which Mr William Jaggard writes:

> 'About the end of the forties I had, I may say, a wholesome dread of meeting 'Jumping Jack' and seeing him bound. About then there was issued from a London house a life of 'Spring-heeled Jack'. It came out in penny weekly numbers, with high illustrations, some of which were loose double-paged pictures in colour. I think the last issue of this marvel was but four or five years ago.'

I can, however, report that the publishers of this first 'life' — the full title of which was *Spring-Heel'd Jack, The Terror of London* were the Newsagents' Publishing Company of 147, Fleet Street. (See illustration facing title page). This long since defunct organisation was a pioneer in the field of these serial publications and maintained a stable of staff writers to pump out serials on every conceivable topic. They enjoyed considerable success with the graphically written and vividly illustrated story of Jack, which their anonymous author based loosely on the newspaper reports —

but much more on his imagination.*

This particular 'Penny Dreadful' like numerous of its contemporaries came in for swift attack from the ever-growing band of moralists who proliferated in the middle and late nineteenth century, attacking virtually every form of entertainment. Such reading — 'penny packets of poison' as one writer dubbed them — were considered not suitable, and indeed positively dangerous, for the masses.

In his essay *A Short Way to Newgate* (1854), newspaper correspondent James Greenwood, who dedicated himself 'towards exposing and extirpating social abuses and those hole-and-corner evils which afflict society' gathered a group of the publications together for review. 'Nasty-feeling, nasty-looking are every one of them,' he said, and then proceeded to denounce them vehemently. His examination of 'Spring Heel'd Jack' is, I think, worth reprinting in full, both because of the attitude it reveals and the precis it gives of an episode from the serial:

> *Spring Heel'd Jack, the Terror of London* is the first on the list. Picture: Jack — with the springs visible at his heels, punching savagely at a policeman's face, and dashing his head against the wall. Summary of contents: Jack indecently assaults a maiden lady, drags her from her bed-chamber by her bed-gown, which is pulled over her head, and finally thrusts her into another bed-room to pass the night with an elderly bachelor gentleman. Somebody springs a rattle, neighbours rouse, bachelor's door forced, bachelor in night garment exposed, and maiden lady dragged nude from beneath bachelor's bed. Next chapter, the loves of a policeman and maid-of-work, and a 'spicy' scene of the pair in the shadow of a tomb in a church yard at midnight.
>
> Says the policeman: 'You lets them catamarans (the girl's mistresses) frighten you from doing your duty, you does.' 'My

* It has been suggested to me by an expert on old boys' magazines that Edwin J. Brett (1828-1895) a journalist who later became a very successful publisher may have authored the series as he wrote a number of the popular penny publications for the Newsagents' Publishing Company at this time. He had a particular penchant for crime stories and enjoyed great popularity with serials like *The Wild Boys of London*. This later encouraged him to launch his own magazine, *Boys of England* which ran for many years and first published the seemingly endless adventures of the notorious Jack Harkaway. Brett eventually became one of the wealthiest publishers of boys' papers, but because of his somewhat arrogant nature it is not surprising to find that he denied or covered up much of his early hack work.

duty?' 'Yes.' 'What duty?' 'What duty, Peggy? Can you look me in the face and ask the question?' 'I don't know what you mean.' 'You don't?' 'No.' 'I do.' 'What is it?' Bristles placed his hand beneath his belt, and heaved a deep sigh. 'Don't you tumble?' he asked. 'No.' 'Then you is green.' 'What do you mean, Mr Bristles?' asked the girl in surprise. 'Mean? Oh! dull of comprehension!' 'I know I am.' 'You are.' 'But t'ain't my fault.' 'Not yours; no, no, not at all; but part –, but part,' said Bristles shaking his head sadly. 'Oh, do explain,' said the girl, in a pleading and half terrified tone. 'What can I do? What do you want me to do? What do you ask?'

And, in reply, Mr Bristles makes a joke disgusting enough to provoke the ghost of Lord Campbell, and so the story is left 'to be continued in our next.'

The way the episode is simplified actually reveals more of Greenwood's character than it does of the original scribe and his publishers. Taken out of context it might seem strong stuff; but the incidents were of a kind common enough in the knowledge of the readers for whom the serial was intended. And should those who, on one hand kept the masses in their places so that they could be exploited, take such a tone of moral indignation when others provided them with a little titillating excitement?*

* A later Spring Heeled Jack serial was also roundly attacked in an anonymous article *Penny Fiction* in *The Quarterly Review* of July 1890. The author writes, 'First on the list comes "Spring Heeled Jack, or the Terror of London", No. 2 given away with No. 1, with 'a splendid coloured plate gratis'. The "plate", a coarse woodcut printed on tinted paper, represents a stage-coach crowded with affrighted passengers, over whose heads springs the devil with horns, hoofs, tail and bat-like wings complete. The story is what might be expected – a tale of highwaymen, murderers, burglars, wicked noblemen, and lovely and persecuted damsels, whose physical charms and voluptuous embraces are dilated upon with exceeding unction. It is almost needless to say that the highwaymen of the romance are not the sorry and sordid rogues we know them to have been in real life, but always "dashing", "high-spirited" and "bold". As a matter of course, they all carry pistols, which they use with unerring skill, which never miss-fire, and apparently never require re-loading. It is equally a matter of course that the enemies of these gallant fellows – the constables, who at the time of the story, which is left in uncertainty, but is presumably about the middle of the Eighteenth Century, are under the orders of a "Commissioner" – are ugly, stupid, ill-conditioned, and cowardly; that it is a "paternal government" under which "things have reached such a pitch that a man may be fined perhaps imprisoned, for carrying a pistol to protect himself"; and that, in one word, all the officers are "tyrants" and oppressors, whom it is the duty of "spirited lads" to resist to the uttermost.'

Such attacks, though, were no deterrent to the 'Penny Dreadful' publishers and in the 1870's another of the Fleet Street coterie revived the Spring Heeled Jack story with even less regard to the 'facts'. The man was Charles Fox, whose premises were just off Fleet Street in Shoe Lane, and who made no bones about he and his writers plagiarizing material for their stories whenever and wherever they saw a likely profit. (Apart from publishing much 'sensational literature', Fox was also the Editor of *The Boy's Standard*, a pioneer magazine for youngsters. He is further credited with having done much to promote the legend of *Sweeney Todd, The Demon Barber of Fleet Street*, when in 1878, he came across an old book on the legend in a second-hand shop and immediately had one of his employees re-write it as a 48-part serial.)

The man who most probably wrote *Spring Heeled Jack, The Terror of London* for Charles Fox was George Augustus Sala, who carried out many similar assignments for the Shoe Lane firm.* Sala began is working life as an illustrator but turned to journalism and augmented his earnings with jobs for publishers like Fox. When later he began contributing to the more distinguished *Illustrated London News* and *Temple Bar*, as well as serving for a period as a foreign correspondent for the *Daily Telegraph*, he tried desperately to cover up his 'Penny Dreadful' work and vehemently denied the authorship of many serials which were clearly his work. Nonetheless he was a writer of imagination and, as in the case of his assignment with *The Terror of London*, capable of adding new dimensions to an existing character.

---

* In an article 'Collecting Penny Dreadfuls — the Literature of Thrills and Horror' in *The Bazaar Exchange and Mart*, January 28, 1936, Barry Ono, the variety star and self-styled 'Penny Dreadful King' said that he then only knew of two complete sets of the Fox Spring Heeled Jack serial still in existence. One of these was his own and he drew on it to describe the story and its characters. He also added as an aside, "Spring Heeled Jack was said to have been a real person and to have stayed at Walton Farm on the Canterbury Road, Folkestone, some fifty years ago." Unfortunately Mr. Ono has been dead for some years, his enormous library of Penny Dreadfuls dispersed (I have actually been fortunate enough to secure a number of items from it for my own collection) and there is seemingly no way we might learn of the background to his intriguing statement. If there is any truth in the claim, the Walton Farm man would appear to have been yet another of the latter-day Spring Heeled Jacks!

Sala's Spring Heeled Jack is a figure endowed with almost supernatural qualities. He has horns growing from his fore-head, piercing eyes and a sinister moustache, and long hair which hangs down his back. He is dressed in a one-piece leotard-like suit and on his arms has black, bat-like wings. Unlike the character on whom he is based, though, he has no springs in his boots.

His character is, however, clearly defined — he is a rescuer of damsels in distress and persecutes those in positions of authority who abuse their power. Sala obviously liked the idea of Jack as a kind of latter-day Robin Hood!

Although there is a complete episode from this serial in the Appendix an extract here would not go amiss, and I think it will indicate another approach in style to the character. Here Jack waylays a coach and confronts a sinister nobleman, Sir Roland Ashton — a man, the author tells us, with 'a soul as black as Satan':

'It so happened that two travellers on the box-seat descended at the 'Three Jolly Wheelers', and Sir Roland and his secretary, Caleb, were quickly accommodated.

In a few minutes the coach rolled off, and in the merry moonlight the horses trotted on swiftly towards Barnet.

For some little while all went well.

But presently, as they neared a part of the road where trees grew thickly on either side, loud, shrill laughter resounded on all sides.

"Ha! ha! ha!"

It seemed to come from all points — behind, in front, on the left, and on the right; now loud and derisive, now shrill, now sonorous and defiant.

A dusky shadow of no particular shape seemed to flit from tree to tree, and mingle with the branches.

Then a strange form went leaping over the wide fields and gambolled in the moonlight.

An awe fell upon all.

Retreat it was useless to talk about.

They must go on, for advance or retire, the fiendish unknown would follow.

Not a word was said.

The driver, alarmed as he was, nevertheless kept his team well in hand, so as to be ready if the horses took fright.

Sir Roland quickly drew a pistol from his breast pocket and

123

waited.

Villain as he was he had abundant courage, and was resolved to put this matter to the test.

Presently, as the coach left the wooded part of the road behind, and came to a part where the hedges were high on either side, there was heard quite close at hand the demon laugh.

"Ha! ha! ha!"

And then, with a whirr and a whizz, Spring Heeled Jack came leaping up towards the sky, clear above the heads of the terrified and astounded travellers, on the summit of the coach.

He looked an awful object, with his bat-like wings outspread, his mouth vomiting forth flame and smoke, his cloven foot showing plainly against the moonlit sky.

The horses, with discordant cries, huddled themselves together on their haunches. The guard, with a yell of terror, fell backwards from his seat, his blunderbus going off in the air as he fell.

Caleb cowered down affrightedly.

Not so Sir Roland.

As the awful apparition sailed up into the air, he rose from his seat, and, raising his pistol, fired point-blank at the figure.

An awful laugh broke from the lips of Spring Heeled Jack.

Then, as he reached the ground again, he leaped once more over the coach, exclaiming, in his most sepulchral tones —

"Ha! ha! Sir Roland Ashton — murderer! You have failed."

This time he again alighted on the summit of the vehicle, where they could see his glaring eyes, his flaming mouth, his red, glossy body, his cloven hoof, and his long, talon-like hands.

Sir Roland, with a groan, fell fainting back upon the seat. The others, unable to look upon the awful being, cowered down and hid their faces.

"Caleb Masters," said the unknown, in a low voice, which sounded as if it were issuing from the tomb, "you have three hundred pounds in a bag in your pocket, belonging, as you think, to your master. Deliver that to me instantly or dread my vengeance. Refuse, and, at a word from me, the whole coach, with its occupants, will be consumed."

And, as he spoke, he breathed forth such a mass of flame and sulphurous smoke that his body was enveloped in vapour, and a suffocating odour pervaded the whole atmosphere.

Caleb raised his head mechanically, and glanced at the terrible apparition.

That glance seemed to fascinate him, and, as if obeying some order that he could not gainsay, he drew from his pocket the bag

Spring Heeled Jack terrorising coach passengers — another 'Penny Dreadful' from the 1870's.

containing the bank-notes and gold, and handed it to Spring-Heeled Jack.

"Ha! ha! ha!" he laughed, as he placed it in a pocket in his wing-like cloak. "Tell Sir Roland I have come this time for some of his ill-gotten gains; next time I will come for his soul."

Then, in a cloud of vapour, which seemed suddenly to envelope him, he disappeared, no one seeing him quit the coach.'

And it was in this manner that Jack's exploits continued for 48 episodes, until at last he bounded dramatically from

125

his final confrontation, sent his weird, ringing laughter back into the faces of his persuers, and disappeared.

In 1904 the Aldine Publishing Company, the latest in a long line of blood and thunder impressarios, revived him again for a short while. This company, which made a speciality of long-running serials based on famous adventure characters — they wrote their own stories of Robin Hood and Dick Turpin and imported ready-made material about Buffalo Bill and Deadwood Dick from America — were noted for the vivid and colourful illustrations on the covers of their publications, which also sold for one penny.

The author of *The Spring-heeled Jack Library*, as the new series was called, was a man named Charlton Lea; who was almost certainly an employee of the company and wrote several of their most successful serials. It has been said — with some justification — that Lea did more to weave a halo of romance around such dubious characters as Turpin, Jack Sheppard and Claude Duval than any other writer in this field. His style was a mixture of hair-raising adventures with slapstick comedy and in hindsight it can be seen that this did not always work.

Lea's rip-roaring tales of Spring Heeled Jack followed the traditional pattern of showing him as masked avenger and punisher of evil-doers, but there were some humourous moments as well — usually at the expense of almost imbecilic and invariably incompetent law officers!

However, Aldine either lacked faith in Jack's abilities to sell, or readers were only interested in more established characters, but the series ran for just twelve issues. Again, though, he would not lay still: the comics took him up next.*

* In later life, many of those who had been forbidden to read 'Penny Dreadfuls', not only admitted to having defied such instructions but suffered no adverse effects as a result. J.A. Hammerton in *Books and Myself* was typical of many when he wrote, 'Not that I could have been consciously critical of the crudities of such stuff as Sweeney Todd, Three-String Jack, or Spring Heeled Jack. . . But it pleases me to think that these stories — notably the Jack Harkaway Series, in which a robust humour was an ingredient — wrought not one per cent of the harm to their boy-readers that the Gangster films have done to the boys of the last quarter of a century.' And George Sampson in *Seven Essays* confessed he also could not resist Harkaway, Sweeney Todd and Spring Heeled Jack and was convinced, 'There was no harm in any of them.'

Although there had been humorous cartoon papers since the 1830's, it was not until 1884 that the first true comic, *Ally Sloper's Half-Holiday* was born. Sloper was a red-nosed, vulgar layabout and his comic a mixture of strip cartoon, jokes and funny pictures, aimed primarily at young working men rather than children. It was only six years later, however that Alfred Harmsworth (later Lord Northcliffe), launched *Comic Cuts*, price ½d, and aimed very much at children. Harmsworth made his intentions quite clear with this proud boast, 'No more Penny Dreadfuls! These healthy stories of Mystery, Adventure, etc., will kill them!'

Scathing though he may have been of these predecessors, Harmsworth and his staff were not above appropriating characters from them for their own use. Robin Hood, Dick Turpin, Buffalo Bill, Sweeney Todd & Co., were all soon appearing in the new comics. Spring Heeled Jack, for his part, first appeared, slightly disguised in 1899, as 'The Human Bat' in *The Funny Wonder*, a ½d comic published on Sundays.

'The Human Bat' was described thus in an encounter with one of his early victims:

'Suddenly, from the very midst of the deep shadow there sprang a strange, weird form. Blacker even than its surroundings, this uncanny object seemed to leap, like a gigantic toad, directly in his path. He jumped forward to encounter it. Springing into the air it vanished.'

The serial about this pseudo-Jack was to last for almost two years, and he was eventually unmasked as the local Police Inspector!

The Funny Wonder was a mixture of text and pictures, but *Illustrated Chips* which followed shortly afterwards was all cartoons, and the popularity of the Spring Heeled Jack legend was clearly demonstrated in the issue of September 9, 1899, when the comic's two famous front-page characters, Weary Willie and Tired Tim took on the agile terror. As you can see from the strip, which is reproduced on page 131, there is a nice complement paid to 'The Human Bat' in the first panel.

It was Harmsworth's rival, the Scottish comic publisher, James Henderson, who contributed the first comic agile terror with 'Larkheeled Jack' who appeared for several years in the weekly *Sparks* from 1917 onwards. This Jack wore a large schoolmaster's mortar board and boots with springs in the heels and made a speciality of playing pranks on tramps and policemen: the two favourite figures of fun in comics at this time.

But Jack was no joke to everyone: that most famous of detectives, Sexton Blake, along with his assistant, Tinker, took him on in *Union Jack* in October 1929. Once more he was terrorising rural districts and it took the intrepid Blake no end of trouble to finally unmask him as a circus stunt artist with a grudge against the world named Waldo the Wonder Man! He was also featured in a Blake story *The Seven Dead Matches Mystery* when the sleuth had moved into *Detective Weekly* in 1933.

The Grey Bat was another mystery crook whose origins could be traced to Spring Heeled Jack, and who was featured in *The Boys' Friendly Library* of August 1929. However, like the donkey man, Rylands, who was unmasked by some schoolboys in Harleigh Severne's story, *Chums*, 'The Bat' was also brought to justice, after all the efforts of the police and authorities had failed, by two intrepid boys!

'The Human Bat' — *a serial story based on the legend of Spring Heeled Jack in* The Funny Wonder, *1899.*

Left 'The Grey Bat' — *another mystery crook whose origins could be traced to Spring Heeled Jack. He found his match in two lads in* The Boy's Friend Library, *August 1929.*

Right Sexton Blake meets Spring Heeled Jack in 'Terror by Night!' *in* Union Jack, *October, 1929.*

The agile terror was again pitted against Sexton Blake in 'The Seven Dead Matches Mystery', *a story in* Detective Weekly *of May 27, 1933.*

A WILD NIGHT'S ADVENTURE WITH SPRING-HEELED JACK.

One of Jack's many comic appearances – Illustrated Chips,
September 1899.

'Spring Heeled' Jack Parkes, outleaping Jumping Jimi, The Victor's super striker (1975).

The spring-heeled businessman — from a Daily Telegraph advertisement, March 1975.

And so the story has continued to the present day, Jack emerging regularly in various metamorphosis. Even while I was working on this book, he appeared yet again — this time in the very contemporary form of a footballer! Readers of *Victor* in February 1975 were puzzled at why their super striker, Jumping Jimi, an eight-foot-tall African who played for Chidsea 'the famous First Division football club', was being beaten in the air by Jack Parkes, the centre half of their great rivals, Ippsley Town. The answer was simple; the man had springs in his heels — and the solution was equally simple, Jumping Jimi became a Spring Heeled Jack himself. But in no time at all the other teams began copying the idea, too!

Fortunately for all footballers, professional and amateur, the Football Association quickly investigated the matter and decided that such boots were illegal. The thought of a nation of football-playing Spring Heeled Jacks was perhaps too much for anyone to contemplate!

Jack has also featured occasionally in advertising, usually in connection with shoes and personal insurance, and again as I was working on this book he turned up in a full page advertisement in *The Daily Telegraph* in March 1975. The advertisement had been placed by the Thomson Organisation promoting their Common Market Telephone Directory. It informed exporters that the best way of getting their name and products before a world wide audience was in the Directory. In the accompanying illustrations eight different methods by which people were advised *not* to tackle this problem were shown — and there, heading the list, was a businessman in. . . . yes, the equipment of Spring Heeled Jack!

Jack does, of course, occasionally warrant a footnote in histories of crime, but has never, before this book, been the subject of a full length study. Articles and essays have, however, occasionally looked into his exploits and these have helped me considerably in my research and are acknowledged where they are quoted.

He springs up from time to time in mystery novels and thrillers too, and while there would be no point in quoting each and every instance, let me just give you a typical example and in doing so underline how his memory is always somewhere in the consciousness of the best writers in the genre. The paragraph is from the late John Dickson Carr's outstanding mystery, *It Walks by Night* (1930) about a night-monster stalking Paris:

> Famous murders! The table piled with roses put the idea into Vautrelle's mind of Landru decorating the room for his sweetheart; we talked of Troppman, of Basson, Vacher, Crippen and Spring-heel Jack; of Major Armstrong and his hypodermic needle and Smith with his tin baths; of Durrant, Haarmann, and La Pommerais; of Cream, Thurtell, and Hunt; of Hoche and Wainwright the poisoners, and the demure Constance Kent. . . There we sat, with that insane repulsion which makes men go into the thing, and Vautrelle talked of the 'artistry of crimes planned like a play', and laughed. . .

There has been just one film about the Spring Heeled Jack legend, and it was primarily based on the W.G. Wills' play for the Lyceum Theatre which I mentioned earlier in this chapter. The film was entitled *The Curse of the Wraydons* and was made just after the Second World War by Ambassador Films. It starred the Master of British Melodrama himself, Tod Slaughter.

Today the film is forgotten, and Tod Slaughter is remembered by only a few die-hard cinema enthusiasts. This is a double tragedy, for the film is a typical period melodrama well worth reviving, and Slaughter deserves a place among the stars of horror and thriller films.

Tod Slaughter, whose real name was Norman Carter Slaughter and could claim direct descent from Captain Cook, was born in Newcastle-on-Tyne in 1885. At the age of 16 he was already in the theatre as an assistant stage manager, and shortly thereafter got his first part in melodrama at the princely sum of 15s. per week. It was not, though, until he was 21 that he got his first speaking role in *The Wrecker of Men* and began his career as 'the most lovable multi-murderer on the British stage' to quote the *Daily Mail.*

During his career which extended over half a century

he appeared in more than 500 plays and sketches, most of which were gruesome affairs in which the villain was always of the blackest, the hero of the noblest, and the heroine of the sweetest — and he was always the grateful target of every boo and hiss.

In 1912 he became an actor-manager and transferred innumerable West End plays to the theatres and variety halls across the country and, said the *Daily Mail,* 'there was hardly a town or village where he had not left his trail of property blood'.

'Few actor managers have done more to keep the lamp of melodrama burning in the theatre,' *The Times* said in a tribute to him. 'A mere catalogue of some of the outstanding titles will recall to older playgoers many hours of horror and suspense which they spent with Tod Slaughter in the West End, the suburbs and the provinces.'

There was a golden era of gore, said the paper, when he was in control of the Elephant and Castle Theatre in London and thousands of playgoers crossed the river each night to see him revel in the horrors of *Maria Marten; or, The Murder in the Red Barn, Sweeney Todd* and *Spring Heeled Jack.* After this he moved on and added other villains such as Long John Silver, Landru, and Burke and Hare to his repertoire of *Grand Guignol* plays.

In hindsight there is little doubt that his most famous role was as Sweeney Todd. *The News Chronicle* commented in their obituary in 1956, 'Over four thousand times as Sweeney Todd he severed jugulars and brought horror to the faces of his audience as rich-red cochineal spurted from his property razor. Many people in and out of the theatre called him Sweeney because he was so identified with the role.'

Later, he adapted this melodrama, and several others, for the films, and won a whole new following.

His performance as Spring Heeled Jack both on the stage, and when he repeated the role on film, is like Sweeney Todd, dashing, blood curdling and full of the murder and menace for which he was famous.

The script for the Ambassador film, made at Bushey Studios by their veteran director Victor M. Gover, was by

Tod Slaughter — the Spring Heeled Jack of Stage and Screen.

Michael Barringer and based on Wills' original melodrama. The story is set during the Napoleonic era and concerns a 'crazy' inventor named Philip Wraydon who is banished from England after an attempted assault on his brother George's wife, Rose. Consumed with hatred for England and his aristocratic family, he decides to help Napoleon and returns home as a spy. To aid him in his undercover work, he designs and makes a pair of spring heeled boots which enable him to

Rare still of the making of 'The Curse of the Wraydons'.

The French spy Wraydon (Tod Slaughter), attempting to gain information by subterfuge.

Wraydon in his other role as Spring Heeled Jack plots a terrible fate for the young girl who has fallen into his clutches.

Slaughter as Spring Heeled Jack attempts to polish off another victim. But retribution awaits him in one of his own inventions.

137

bound from one place to another, always keeping one jump ahead of his persuers.

To further his espionage, Wraydon ruthlessly strangles all those who cross his path — both men and women — and pins the murders on his handsome officer nephew, Captain Jack Clayton played by a youthful Bruce Seton. This stalwart servant of king and country battles all obstacles to clear his name and finally manages to turn the tables on Philip Wraydon — the 'Spring Heeled assailant' dies in one of his own diabolical contraptions.*

Tod Slaughter entered into the role of the cunning Wraydon with all his usual panache, and the film trade's magazine, *Picture Show* was quick to single him out for praise in its May 1946 pre-release review:

'The picture, an earnest attempt to revive lusty Lyceum days, lags at the start — there is far too much dallying in the chequered hero's regimental mess — but luckily the villain of the piece, played with gusto by Tod Slaughter, finally makes his presence felt and stages an exciting last minute rally. The concluding episodes borrow with good effect much of the gory glory of *Sweeney Todd* . . . The star, still a big draw out of town, should get the film over in his home territory.'

And indeed Tod Slaughter as Spring Heeled Jack did 'get the film over' although such were its contents that the Censor felt obliged to categorise it 'A' for adults. Sadly, though, after a run through the country which lasted for almost a year, it dropped from sight and there are probably no more than one or two prints still existing today. †

---

* The other stars of the 94 minute picture which was produced by Gilbert Church were Barry O'Neill as George Wraydon, Pearl Cameron as Rose Wraydon, Alan Lawrance as George Heeningham, Gabriel Toyne as Lieutenant Payne, and Lorraine Clews as Helen Sedgefield.

† Denis Gifford, the film and comic historian, who was kind enough to help me with information for this chapter, says that an extract from the film was subsequently used in a later picture, *A Ghost for Sale* made in 1952. He also informs me that Spring Heeled Jack appeared briefly as a character in the German film *Waxworks* made by Paul Leni in 1924. Conrad Veidt played Jack as a waxwork in a Chamber of Horrors, who is brought to life in the storyteller's fantasies.

Two years later Slaughter made a film based on the Burke and Hare murders, but this time the Censor found his ghoulish grave-robbing just too much and the picture was refused a release certificate until the two leading characters had been re-named Moore and Hart (sic) and the picture re-titled *The Greed of William Hart*.

For the remainder of his career he returned to the stage, and continued to delight audiences with his line 'Oh, I'd love to polish you off!' hissed at anyone foolish enough to interrupt him when in full flood.

Perhaps as he would have wished, Tod Slaughter died in February 1956 after giving one of his finest performances as William Corder, the villain, in *The Murder in the Red Barn* at Derby. He was almost 71 years old and, as always, had made his final curtain call being hanged in full view of a silent, chilled and absolutely enthralled audience.

That night the last of the great Victorian melodramatic stars passed on — and no other actor since has been quite able to gloat as well, or polish off his victim with such a terrifying smile. He undoubtedly performed a service in reviving Sweeney Todd, Spring Heeled Jack and all the rest — and now I believe deserves the same for his films and his own memory.

8

Was Jack a Man from Outer Space?

William Henry Street in the Everton district of Liverpool was a typical road of red-bricked terraced houses of the kind to be found in many of the industrial towns of Lancashire in the early years of the twentieth century. The people who lived there were, in the main, hard-working folk, down-to-earth in their approach to life and not given to flights of fancy. Some were employed in the local factories, others further afield in the Liverpool docks; all knew the fears of unemployment with the fluctuating commercial fortunes of this part of the country.

It was in this perhaps unlikely setting that Spring Heeled Jack leapt into the twentieth century.

As we have seen in the last chapter, Jack was a wide-spread figure in the middle years of the nineteenth century. After the seventies, however, his appearances became much less frequent, and often the reports themselves are of dubious origins. Clearly, too, the disguise was being utilised by numerous different people and only those which took place in the same localities and within short spaces of time of each other were the work of one man. It is inconceivable to me that anyone like the Marquis of Waterford was abroad moving from one locality to the next, generating a new reign of terror. No, the widely scattered incidents were the handiwork of individual pranksters seeking to do little more than get some perverse pleasure by springing out on unsuspecting victims and in doing so preserved the legend of the agile terror.

Some of the reports indicate that these later Spring Heeled Jacks made only the most rudimentary attempts to create the disguise and spring-heeled boots of the original. They merely pounced out from hiding places on passers-by, and because everyone *knew* such exploits were bound to be the work of Spring Heeled Jack, so they became. It mattered not that there were no fiery eyes or mouth vomiting flame; no flowing cloak or seven league boots.

But the exploits which occurred in the area of William Henry Street in September 1904 bore all the hall-marks of the old Jack.

The autumn of that year was cold and damp, and once the residents of the street had returned from their work, nights were spent before the fire rather than in going out. At first, the shadows which seemed to pass so quickly across the windows of the houses at the lower end of William Henry Street were thought to be folk hurrying home. No one took much notice.

Then one evening a Mrs Hudson happened to pull aside a curtain just after a particularly large shadow had been reflected into her room. Almost opposite her house a gas street lamp flickered in the gloom, the light reflecting off the damp cobbles of the roadway.

She peered down the street, her eyes narrowing. Then she raised her hand to her mouth in amazement. A shape rather like a giant bat was just about to turn the corner at the end.

She looked harder, but in an instant the figure was gone.

Puzzled, Mrs Hudson let the curtain fall back into place. Had her eyes been playing tricks? Had she seen some kind of huge figure leaping down the road? Her commonsense told her not; but the evidence of her eyes seemed to deny this.

Mrs Hudson said nothing about the matter to her family that evening, nor to her neighbours the following day. But that night she was at her curtains again. At exactly the same time, just after nine o'clock, the figure bounded down the street once more.

This time Mrs Hudson was in no doubt; her startled eyes watched a man wearing a flowing cloak and high-heeled black boots spring down the street with a series of mighty bounds. But even when the figure disappeared from view, Mrs Hudson still decided to say nothing to her family.

The next day, though, she found she was not the only one to have seen the figure, or vision, or whatever it was. The whole street was alive with gossip, and Mrs Hudson was gratified to have confirmation of her own fears.

'Must 'ave bin Spring Heeled Jack' one old codger announced to his cronies as they stood talking at the corner of the street. 'Recall my father talking about 'im when I was a young 'un. A real terror 'e was then,' the man went on.

And so by lunch time on that day all of Everton, and much of Liverpool, knew that Spring Heeled Jack was back on the prowl again.

The more sceptical were inclined to disbelieve the reports. Times had changed, people were not so superstitious now, nor were busy streets in the heart of built-up areas the normal venues for this agile terror – or so they thought.

But that night, Spring Heeled Jack confounded his critics by appearing yet again, bounding down the street before a row of wide-eyed faces pressed against the glass panes of their windows. 'Jumped twelve foot in the air,' voiced one man. 'Leaped a good ten foot at each bound,' said another. 'Could 'ave cleared a house,' ventured a third.

The next day was a Saturday; the night when quite a lot of the William Henry Street residents normally went out. Even though there was considerable alarm about the apparition in their midst, the more resolute were still determined to have their outing.

Couples who ventured out encountered no problems. But two young girls with the spirit of youth in their blood, and not to be frightened by such tales, walked boldly through the neighbourhood on their way to assignations.

Both regretted their foolhardiness when the masked terror suddenly sprang out from the shadows and flung them to the ground with a cry of laughter. But they were not attacked;

he bounded away almost immediately, and they ran home frightened and badly shaken.

The following week Jack was less in evidence; perhaps because everyone was now on the look out for him. In particular a group of dockers — one of them the father of the attacked girls — were roaming the streets at night with clubs in their hands and vengeance in their hearts. Nonetheless, Jack pounced again on two more women, on separate occasions, in nearby Salisbury Street, and matters began to look rather more serious.

The police had naturally been informed and were also patrolling the district, two constables passing along each street every half hour. The press, both local and national, were showing more than a little interest in the events, and the *News of the World* for September 25 carried the following story:

SPRING HEELED JACK

— Ghost With a Weakness For Ladies

Everton (Liverpool) is scared by the singular antics of a ghost, to whom the name of 'Spring Heeled Jack' has been given, because of the facility with which he has escaped, by huge springs, all attempts of his would-be captors to arrest him.

William Henry Street is the scene of his exploits, and crowds of people assemble nightly to see them, but only a few have done so yet, and 'Jack' is evidently shy. He is said to pay particular attention to ladies.

So far the police have not arrested him, their sprinting powers being inferior.

There was something a little light-hearted about the *News of the World* piece, almost as if they failed to credit the story. Jack himself may have taken offence, for the following week he carried out his most extraordinary prank to date.

One afternoon, in broad daylight, as people were returning home from work, he suddenly bounded into full view in William Henry Street. With a ringing laugh, he sprang by the startled populace, up one side of the street and down the other.

Before the first wide-eyed person could make a move to catch him, says a contemporary report, Jack bounded a good 25 feet from the roadway onto a rooftop. He then leapt over the roofs to adjacent Stitt Street and then across Haigh Street.

For a moment he paused, a dark figure silhouetted amongst the chimney pots, then turned and jumped across the shingles to Salisbury Street. Doors and windows clattered open as the word of this amazing performance passed from house to house. Spring Heeled Jack was on their very roof tops!

Again Jack paused, now in full view of over a hundred people. Eyes strained to try and get a better view of his features, but a mask seemed to cover his eyes and his billowing cloak made his limbs difficult to see. Although he had now been visible for the best part of ten minutes, no one was any the wiser as to who he might be.

Then, with another laugh, he sprang down behind a roof — and completely vanished.

Though William Henry Street, the adjacent roads, all of Everton and much of Liverpool was subsequently combed by the police and many suspects interrogated, Spring Heeled Jack had disappeared as completely and as mysteriously as he had arrived.

What kind of man was he — and what were his motives? The questions remain unanswered to this day.

Although there are other scattered reports of sightings of Spring Heeled Jack in the early years of this century, the exploits at Everton were in all probability the last occasion when he made himself known to the population of Britain in a major way. Time was passing his kind by — he was part of another age and any glamour that might have been attached to his flouting of the law had long since been dissipated. The First World War in fact saw his final demise as an active figure — there are not even rumours after that date*

---

* Interestingly, I came across a reference about spring heeled boots during the Second World War. Apparently the Germans tried to take the shock out of landing for their parachute troops by experimenting with springs in the heels of the soldiers' boots. Their design, unfortunately, must have lacked the ingenuity of Jack's, for they reported an 85 per cent incidence of broken ankles and promptly abandoned the project!

His name, though, did crop up in two further instances which are well worth relating as they indicate the durability of his legend.

The first instance concerns a remarkable negro who worked on the canal system at Cassiobury Park and was said to be able to leap across the fourteen-foot canal at a single bound!

Marc Alexander relates the story in his book, *Phantom Britain* (1975):

> The negro was in the employment of the local landowner when the canal was first cut, and once it was in operation it amused him to terrorise the boatmen. Being 'as black as the very night itself' he boarded moored narrow-boats under the cover of darkness and stole the lock keys (or windlasses) which were used to open the sluices.
>
> Superstitious canal folk believed it was a ghost which played such tricks upon them until an enraged skipper caught Jack in the act and killed him with his lock key. When an old hollow tree in the park was struck by lightning some years ago it was found to be filled with two hundred of these keys which the Negro had stolen.

The man's nickname, as you may well have suspected, was 'Spring Heeled Jack', and Mr Alexander concludes his story, 'It is ironical that black Jack, who enjoyed playing at being a ghost, now has the reputation for being a real one. If you are planning a canal holiday make sure that when you reach beautiful Cassiobury Park you keep a wary eye on your lock key!'

Spring Heeled Jack's name also arose in another connection in 1929 when a number of dogs were found poisoned in Lancashire and Cheshire. There seemed no particular reason for these heartless killings — the dogs concerned were not known to be ferocious or difficult animals — but all were discovered by their owners stretched out rigid after having eaten poisoned meat.

And beside each lay a crudely scribbled note that more poisonings were to follow. They were all signed 'Spring Heeled Jack'.

The authorities were at a loss to know what had prompted

these indiscriminate killings, or what the poisoner sought in order to cease his activities.

The Morning Post of October 19 commented on the matter in its 'Way of the World' column:

> The dog poisoning scare in Lancashire and Cheshire has been revived by notices threatening more of this cruel practice, and signed by 'Spring Heeled Jack'. There can be few people now alive who remember the original bearer of that name who created a reign of terror in London suburbs during the first year of Queen Victoria's reign.'

The paper went on to recapitulate the facts about Jack and added finally:

> As the tales of outrage grew, so did that of the remarkable powers of Spring Heeled Jack. He could leap thirty feet or so at a bound, and was clearly no ordinary mortal, if, indeed, he were of this world at all.
>
> Today he seems to be forgotten, save for the occasional use of his name by evil-doers, but in his day he was a bogey of whom the terror kept many a woman indoors after dark.

The Morning Post's doubtless flippant comment about whether Spring Heeled Jack was 'of this world at all' brings me conveniently to the final topic I wish to discuss about the legend of this remarkable figure. It is the question which has been posed: 'Was Jack actually a visitor from outer space?'

At first sight, that might seem a totally absurd suggestion. Yet it has been carefully argued in a leading magazine studying the phenomena known as Unidentified Flying Objects (UFO's), or 'Flying Saucers' to give them their popular label. And when many people of distinction and reason — not the least of them being American President Jimmy Carter who claims to have actually seen a UFO — give serious credence to this whole area of inquiry, I think the theory has a place in this book.

The argument was presented in the May-June 1961 issue of *Flying Saucer Review* in an article entitled, 'The Mystery of Springheel Jack' by a regular contributor, J. Vyner.

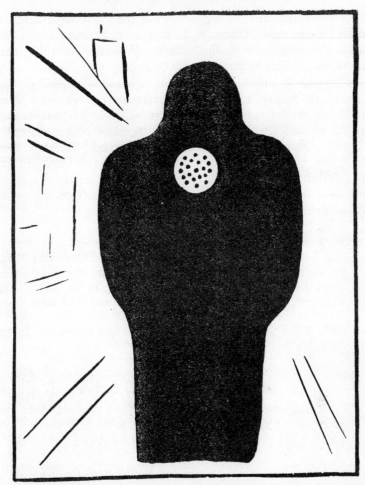

Spring Heeled Jack — a man from space? A drawing from
Flying Saucer Review, *1961.*

Waveney Girvan, a leading expert on UFO's and the magazine's editor, introduced the article by relating that in a
previous issue he had called for evidence of extra-terrestrials
in our midst as a check on the stories put forward by a
number of people who claimed to have contacted men from
other worlds. 'This challenge aroused considerable interest,'
he went on, 'and has produced both modern and historical
evidence. In the following article the author suggests that a

147

notorious and almost legendary figure may have been a visitor from outer space. The facts in this article are taken from contemporary accounts and have been checked against all available records for accuracy.'

Mr Vyner's article begins by concisely reviewing the history of Spring Heeled Jack from the day in November 1837 when the lanes and commons around London began to be stalked by 'an uncatchable monster of superhuman powers, easily evading detection and arrest.' He describes how the matter was not publicised until the Lord Mayor of London raised the matter in a somewhat sceptical way — and was deluged with information. The descriptions given of the man, says Mr Vyner, were all identical:

> The intruder was tall, thin and powerful. He had a prominent nose, and bony fingers of immence power which resembled claws. He was incredibly agile. He wore a long, flowing cloak, of the sort affected by opera-goers, soldiers and strolling actors. On his head was a tall, metallic-seeming helmet. Beneath the cloak were close-fitting garments of some glittering material like oilskin or metal mesh. There was a lamp strapped to his chest. Oddest of all: the creature's ears were cropped or pointed like those of an animal.

Mr Vyner goes on to describe how London became gripped in a reign of terror, and examines certain of Spring Heeled Jack's attacks, beginning with that of Jane Alsop at Bow on February 20 1838. He has his own particular version of what happened when Jack confronted the girl on her doorstep:

> Miss Alsop screamed, and only then did the visitor become hostile. He siezed her arm in an iron grip of clawlike fingers, but one of her sisters came hurriedly to the rescue. Jack at once spurted balls of fire into the girl's face and fled, leaving her unconscious. In his flight, Jack apparently dropped his cloak, which was immediately snatched up by another person lurking in the shadows, who sped after him and was lost to sight in the darkness.
>
> All accounts of this episode agree that there was a wanton attack on Jane Alsop, but the facts do not bear out this theory. Before her screams roused the household, Jack made no attempt to molest the girl. Indeed, her reaction seems to have come as a shock to him. Was he expecting to be received as a friend?

Two days earlier, though not revealed until after the Old Ford incident had made headlines, a Miss Scales, of Limehouse, was walking through Green Dragon Alley. The alley was a dim-lit passage beside a public house, and when she saw a tall figure lurking in the shadows Miss Scales hesitated, waiting for her sister who had fallen behind.

The sister, who described the loiterer as 'tall, thin and (save the mark) gentlemanly,' came up in time to see his long cloak thrown aside, and a lantern flashing on the startled girl. There was no time to scream; Jack's weird blue flame spurted into his victim's face and she dropped to the ground in a deep swoon. Whereupon, Jack walked calmly away.

There is a suggestion here that Springheel Jack had a rendezvous in Green Dragon Alley. Possibly he was waiting for that companion who had retrieved his cloak at Old Ford. Conceivably, he was to meet, by appointment, some contact who would take him to the safe house he had been seeking for the past three months.

Mr Vyner is now deeply into his argument that Jack was not human, but a man from another world. He says, too, that Jack was nearing the end of his anabasis and, after the incident with Mr Ashworth's servant lad at his house in the Commercial Road, he vanished from London 'as abruptly as if the earth had swallowed him up.'

The author believes that the police were only too happy to see the back of him and to drop the case without, as he puts it, 'ever having troubled to ask the obvious questions'. He maintains that it was hoaxers who thereafter invoked Jack's name. (Interestingly, he mentions the Marquis of Waterford as a possible suspect but although his 'doings were wild and extravagant enough' they were always 'tempered with a rough good humour'. Mr Vyner rather blandly exonerates him from all blame with the phrase, 'terrorising a countryside and scaring old ladies was not characteristic of him!')

Mr Vyner now begins to draw still more startling conclusions from the evidence.

'There is no comment, anywhere (he writes) on coincidences. But it is notable that, within a radius of less than a mile, Jack paid two visits and was encountered once within the space of

149

ten days. This is the pattern of intention, of purpose. Immediately Jack localised his activities all trace of him was lost. I suggest that a contact had been made.

'Unremarked by contemporaries: that in the metropolis — perhaps nowhere else — was triplicity of Green Dragon Alleys or Passages, duplication of Turner Streets. That in the distortion of the unfamiliar names like Ashworth and Alsop may sound familiar.

'Unknown to 1838: Aircrew, baled out over hostile territory. Strange the suggestion of evasion, living off the land, stealing clothes and food. Hard to find the safe house where lives the agent who can put them on the road to home.

'Known to 1838: Springheel Jack — tearing clothes from men's backs, stealing the pieman's stock. Whose outlandish uniform passes muster only by night. Who bases himself in parks where game abounds.'

Such is the basis of Mr Vyner's argument. I am afraid though, there are a number of discrepancies in his interpretation of the 'facts' — as the reader will no doubt be aware from already having read about the instances quoted in much greater detail — but this does not stop the theory being a fascinating and intriguing one. Nor is Mr Vyner finished — for he believes that the visitor from another world whom he calls Spring Heeled Jack has been reappearing on earth fairly regularly ever since.

He prefaces this part of his theory with what he calls 'the final escape of Spring Heeled Jack from his incarnation of 1837-38' and writes as follows:

'Inspector Hemer of the Liverpool police may unwittingly have witnessed the final escape of Springheel Jack from his incarnation of 1837-38. He was patrolling the long boundary of Toxteth Park, near Liverpool, on the night of July 6, 1838. A vivid flash of 'lightning' drew his attention to a great ball of fire which hung motionless over a nearby field.

'The object remained stationary for about two minutes, then, emitting showers of brilliant sparks, it sank swiftly to the ground and disappeared. The Inspector wheeled his horse about, and rode away from his chance of apprehending England's most-wanted character.'

Mr Vyner says that Inspector Hemer's reactions show that 'policemen and flying saucers haven't much changed in the past hundred and fifty years'. Nor, he believes, has Spring Heeled Jack and he maintains that the isolated encounters reported at intervals through the intervening years 'suggest a run ashore to stretch cramped limbs after days of close confinement'.

He proposes Jack's encounter with the two sentries at Aldershot Army Camp in 1877 as an instance of this. 'He soared over the heads of two sentries posted by the magazine,' he writes, 'landing noiselessly beside them. Both men fired without effect, whereupon Jack stunned them with a burst of his blue fire and made off.'

Mr Vyner has a theory about this 'blue fire'. He asks:

'Is this blue fire a stupefying gas? Or is it the visible product of a magnetic effect transmitted along a beam of polarised light from Jack's mysterious lantern? Intense magnetic fields produce effects comparable to those experienced by Jack's victims — and by those who have ventured too near grounded saucers. Though the inverse square law governing radiation is commonly thought to prevent development of paralysing ray devices small enough to be easily portable, a concentrated beam might trigger off a magnetic disturbance in the vicinity of its target.'

Naturally enough, Mr Vyner is also anxious to try and explain that oldest of mysteries about Jack — how he achieves the enormous leaps which have made him a legend. His solution is quite remarkable:

'The enigma of Springheel Jack's astounding leaps is, like the siren's song, not entirely beyond conjecture. It is possible that a being from a high-gravity planet might be able to duplicate some of his feats on our own; likewise, there is the possibility of his employing an individual rocket device, such as U.S. Army engineers have developed. Such a device can carry a man over wide rivers and standing trees, but what happens on landing?

'All the accounts of Jack's feats seem to indicate that he had perfect control over his mighty bounds. In fact, his silent landings indicate buoyancy. The buoyancy of the balloon-jumper with a gasbag attached to shoulder harness. But, despite observations of Jack's 'carrying something on his back', I am inclined to think

151

tne solution must lie in the possession of a device for neutralising gravity. Normally, the user would reduce his weight to a point at which he could walk normally while retaining the capacity for tremendous leaps. Increasing the power would enable him to soar, or even float. But he would then lose control. . . unless he had wings. Light, collapsible wings, serving as control surfaces, requiring little muscular effort to use.'

Perhaps the most remarkable part of Mr Vyner's article is that which he saves until the last. For it is his conviction that this Jack-from-outer-space has not only appeared in Britain, but has been seen in America as well. Again he marshalls his facts from the voluminous UFO files:

'In 1944, towards the end of August, Springheel Jack appeared at Mattoon, Illinois, U.S.A. In this incarnation, he appeared by night at open windows, as if in search of someone known to him by sight. Those who saw him — mainly women — were left stunned by a device pointed at them which made consciousness dissolve in a fiery whirl. This time, however, a strange, cloying smell was left behind in the room he had entered.

'For nearly a month Jack flitted through the bedrooms of Mattoon with the energy of a Groucho Marx. Then, as suddenly as he had come, he disappeared in a night of strange and widespread hysteria. Such phenomena, indeed, as have been associated with intense magnetic disturbance — or with saucer landings. The hysteria did not, however, spread to the wall of state and local police who encircled the town so that no human being should have been able to evade their dragnet. Possibly Jack soared over their heads as he had done many times in the past.'

Nor, says the author, are these the only instances of his appearance in America. He cites, but does not go into details, the strange manifestations reported at Louisville, Kentucky on July 28, 1880; at Chehalis, Washington on January 6 1948 and Houston, Texas, on June 18, 1953 when he was allegedly seen sitting in a Pecan tree!

I have looked into these instances myself, but find little to link them with Spring Heeled Jack — though the interested reader may spot more than I did! Whatever the outcome, if a case can be made for his having appeared on the other side of the Atlantic, his prowess would seem to be even more remarkable than we thought! And just where else might he choose to appear next?

So, finally, who then is, or was, Spring Heeled Jack? Mr Vyner admits the problem still remains, although he has considerable faith in his theory. If he was an imposter, he maintains, then he was at least a super-imposter who carried a super-weapon — a raygun.

We have, I believe, found many of the answers in these pages — but not every one. Like all the very best mysteries, there are still questions that need settling about the life and legend of this extraordinary figure. I hope there will be those who will come up with new facts from fresh sources about him — and there may well be exploits I have overlooked still awaiting discovery in the files of old newspapers. I have no doubt there will be those who will disagree with some of my findings, for this is another of those stories about which opinions can wax furious. Who knows, a Jack the Ripper-type *cause celebre* may yet grow around Spring Heeled Jack?

In any event, one can only marvel that a figure who sprang out of the shadows beside a lonely cemetary on the outskirts of London nearly a century and a half ago should still be such an enigma. And not only an enigma, but a household name wherever the English language is spoken. Whatever Spring Heeled Jack may or may not have been, there is no denying him that accolade.

Boxford, Suffolk
May 1977

Springheeled Husband
Pounced on Lovers

An irate husband flew into action on a homemade catapault when he saw his wife being cuddled by another man.

He made a springboard out of a long plank and two car tyres and after a run launched himself into the air.

He crashed head-first through the kitchen window of the house where his wife was being cuddled.

Mr Michael Garratt, prosecuting, told Dudley, Worcs, Crown Court, that the husband landed in the sink and gently slid to the floor.

Graham Street, 21, of Rowley Regis, near Dudley, pleaded guilty to causing £1.49 damage to the window at the house on the Old Park Farm Estate at Dudley. He was put on probation for two years by the Judge W.R. Davison and told not to 'indulge' in such 'amateur dramatics' again.

Mr John West, defending, said the only person to get hurt was Street. He had no intention of interfering with his wife again.

THE DAILY TELEGRAPH
December 6 1974

154

Appendix:

'Spring Heeled Jack, The Terror of London'

This 'Penny Dreadful' by George Augustus Sala was published by Charles Fox in 48 weekly parts in the 1870's. In this episode, our heroine, Daisy Leigh, whose father has been brutally murdered, has been kidnapped by an evil dwarf named Gedge Foote who hopes to trick her into marriage and thereby secure the fortune she is to inherit. She has been taken to the house of Gedge's female accomplice, a Mrs. Foster, who is concealing her identity by using the name 'Mrs. Barton'. Poor Daisy is, of course, quite unaware of her real position and believes she is among friends. Now read on. . .

For two or three days after her arrival at the pretended Mrs. Barton's (the real Mrs. Foster) Daisy lived an excessively quiet existence.

It was a melancholy one enough, what with the hideously dismal surroundings and the terrible reminiscences of her father's death.

Mrs. Foster was not the best of companions, and, consequently, Daisy spent most of her time in her own room, where the bright sun of August only showed her wastes of ground stretching down to the water's edge, and a few cultivated fields and dreary-looking shanties, while the night generally swallowed up everything in misty darkness.

Mrs. Foster's was a mysterious life altogether.

She had, in fact, no visible means of subsistence.

Apparently she had plenty of money; she rarely ever went out, but the tradesmen called, and she paid them.

But she did nothing for her living.

Occasionally carts would draw up of a night at the door, and loud, rough voices would be heard laughing in uproarious chorus in the side yard, where there were all manner of rough sheds.

She said that her husband was a sea captain, and she had lost sight of him for some years.

At any rate, she had plenty of time on her hand, and would often come of her own accord to gossip.

"What a strange thing it is!" said Daisy one evening, when Mrs. Foster had invited her into her cosy kitchen. "What a strange thing it is that the mysterious person who sent me here has never turned up."

"Mysterious person!" laughed Mrs. Foster. "Why, what on earth do you mean?"

"The person who gave me your address, and told me to come here. I have never seen him since the day of my father's murder, and I long to see him, to thank him, and to hear what plans he proposes to hunt up the assassin."

The woman laughed at her, as if she thought that she was taking leave of her senses.

"Why, what do ye mean?" she cried. "Why, I never! Say you ain't seen him, when he came the other night and brought you here, and stayed to supper, and kissed you when he went away, and all that. Well, I never did!"

Daisy flushed, but still she could not help smiling as she answered —

"Oh! I don't mean him, Mrs. Barton. He's nobody — that poor, ugly dwarf. He's very kind and lent me money, and showed me my way here, and I think he did kiss me. But I forgave him, because, perhaps, he'd had a drop to drink, and was excited."

"Well, look here, Miss Leigh," said Mrs. Foster, emphatically, "there's some very stupid mistake here. In the first place, my name ain't Barton. It's Foster. Poor Mr. Foote! he forgot my name when he told you, and when he came in the afternoon afore you came he said, 'Bless me! if I ain't told my sweetheart your name's so-and-so. Don't be surprised, then, if she calls ye so. If I tell her different, she's so timid, she'll get scared like.' And as for 'poor, ugly dwarf,' I wonder how you can talk like that about a chap you're going to marry, and the banns up and all."

This, considering the shuddering dread the words inspired, was a long speech for Daisy Leigh to listen to.

156

But she suffered Mrs. Foster to proceed and finish, and then broke into a loud, hysterical laugh.

"You are having a good joke at my expense, Mrs. Foster," she said. "In the first place, I have never had a sweetheart, as you call it, in my life. I never had a dozen words with Gedge Foote before the day after my poor father's death; and as for banns, of course, that is your fun, though banns can be nothing to me for many a long, long day. It was not Mr. Foote who bade me come here — it was a person whom I do not know (and she shuddered slightly). And so, since I am in the wrong place, I must get back to the Mint as quickly as I can, or I shall lose my best friend."

She rose as she spoke.

She was resolved to proceed to her own room at once, dress herself, and quit the house, using a few shillings to enable her to reach the Mint, and returning the rest to Gedge Foote at his own place.

Mrs. Foster's laugh alarmed her.

"What is there to laugh at?" she cried.

"Very much, I think."

"What do you mean?"

"You talk of quitting this house?"

"Yes."

"Don't you know you can't?"

"Why not?"

"There isn't a window or a door through which you could escape if you were flying for your life," said Mrs. Foster, with a bland smile. "Once upon a time, ye see, this 'ere place was a madhouse, leastways a private asylum, kept by a doctor; and lor' bless ye, the bolts and bars are that strong it 'ud take half-a-dozen strong men all their time to get through."

"By what right can you detain me?" cried Daisy, drawing up her little body defiantly, her eye flashing, and her bosom heaving.

"By the right given me by Mr. Foote," said Mrs. Foster, flushing and losing her temper. "He brought you here and paid me well, and said I was to take every care of you, and so on; and so you can't leave my house until Mr. Foote says you may."

Daisy had fallen into a trap.

She had suspected it before.

But now she was certain.

What was to be done?

Certainly nothing by being precipitate.

So she would be calm.

"When do you expect Mr. Foote?" she asked.

"Either to-night or to-morrow night," said Mrs. Foster, "and then he isn't going away until the wedding."

"Your talk is absurd, and it annoys me," said Daisy, "You must know that in England a forced marriage is impossible if the girl only has courage."

"Ah! but if you persist in refusing him," said Mrs. Foster, "there is something worse. He will remain under this roof with you until you will be glad to marry him."

Daisy, even without the horrid leer in the woman's eyes, would have known what she meant, and a shuddering thrill passed through her frame.

She passed towards the door.

"I will go to my room now," she said, "and if Mr. Foote makes his insane proposals to me, he will find how I appreciate his madness."

"You had better speak more civilly to him than you do of him," said Mrs. Foster, "or you may find him dangerous. He knows he can do as he likes here."

"And that you would help him in his iniquity." said Daisy.

"Just so."

"I fear you not," said Daisy, defiantly; "no harm will come to me. Heaven will protect the innocent, much as you scoff at my resistance."

And she quitted the room.

As she did so she was in the passage, and with a sudden impulse she flew to the front door.

It was barred and bolted, both bolts and bars being on the inside; but a formidable lock was on the door, in which the key had been turned and removed.

There at any rate there was no escape.

She hurried then into her own room, where she felt certain she had never seen any signs of bars at the windows.

As may be imagined, she dashed impatiently towards the casement.

But there she gave vent to a little cry of dismay.

No one would have suspected the presence of bars.

But there, nevertheless, they were; artfully concealed by creeping plants, which on more than one occasion she had complained of as making the room so dark.

"At any rate I am safe here for a time," she murmered, as she bolted and locked her door.

But as she did so another click told her that by some machinery the room had been locked on the outside as well.

Tears stood in Daisy's eyes.

But her good little heart beat high with brave determination.

"The battle has begun," she said, "but I will never yield with my life. I know not what love is; but whatever it is I could not feel it for such a being as Gedge Foote."

On one thing she was determined.

She would remain on the watch all night, and as far as possible would refrain from food.

She had a suspicion that if she did not take this precaution something might be surreptitiously administered to make her insensible, or, at any rate, to dull her intellect.

She could contrive somewhat to neutralise the effect of anything by only taking the tiniest quantities at a time.

And another thing, she would not undress herself, so as to be ready for flight at any moment.

She had not been in her room long before Mrs. Foster's voice was heard outside, and then a kind of wicket in the wall at the side of the door was pushed open.

"Here is your supper," said the woman.

A savoury smell assailed the girl's nostrils.

But she was resolute.

"Thank you; I am not hungry," returned she.

The woman waited to hear no more, but slammed the little wicket to with a bang.

"All right," she muttered; "perhaps she won't be so cheeky when she's starved herself."

That night Daisy was undisturbed, and on the next likewise.

Loud voices and laughter were heard in the house.

But that was all.

She was used to strange noises in the place, and consequently this did not affect her.

She kept resolutely to her room all the time, and though Mrs. Foster unbolted the door, she never once took advantage of the permission.

Food she took in tiny quantities, just sufficient to keep body and soul together.

On the third night, however, just as she had removed her dress and her boots, to throw herself on her couch for a little rest, there was a knock at the front door, and presently someone entered.

Her room was not locked, and so springing noiselessly towards the door she opened it, and, listened.

"Quite a stranger," said Mrs. Foster to someone.

"Yes, quite. Couldn't get here before," said the familiar voice of Gedge Foote. "How's our young lady?"

"Hush! Don't speak loud. Don't speak here at all," said the woman. "She's turned rumbustious, and you'll have no end of trouble with her."

"I hope not," said Foote; "but let's go into the back parlour."
They were soon out of the passage, and, plucking up her cou-
age, Daisy resolved to go down and listen.

Her bootless feet made little noise on the stairs, and it was not
long before she stood in the front parlour, which was only divided
from the back one by a folding door.

Here she cowered down, and, with eager ears, listened.

"I hope you've not been ill-using her," said Foote. "I didn't
bring her here to be insulted, you know."

"Insulted! Who's insulted her I should like to know?" cried
Mrs. Foster; "only I don't like these upstart wenches."

Gedge laughed.

"Well, you can't expect every girl to like to be treated in this
way," he said; "and then I am not such a fool as to think I'm
handsome."

"Oh! handsome is as handsome does," said Mrs. Foster. "Every
girl can't expect to have her pick and choose, and she's as poor as
poor can be — not got a farthing of her own, and you've been
that generous to her."

"Well, never mind; tell us all that has happened."

The woman did so.

A brightly coloured story it was, too.

Evidently it did not increase Gedge Foote's good humour.

"It's no use trying to escape me," he said. "I've had my eye on
her ever since, a long time ago, I saw her trim little ankle tripping
up the stairs on the Mint, and, hark ye, Mrs. Foster, it isn't only
herself, though I'd be glad of her without a penny."

"What then?"

"Someday she'll be rich."

"How do you know?"

"That's my affair; but whoever marries her marries money.
She won't be able to claim it yet, but she's bound to have it."

"Well, it's all easy enough if you only have pluck."

"How so?"

"Let me put a little sleeping stuff in her tea to-morrow evening;
she'll go off into a fine slumber, and be as quiet as a lamb until
morning. Then you can pay her a visit, and when she finds she
can't help herself she'll go with you to church as ready as can be."

Daisy shuddered, and pressed her hands over her tremulous
bosom.

Innocent of the world's ways as she was she had yet expected
something of this kind; but she was not prepared for Gedge's
answer.

"No, no! That won't do for me," he said; "it might do with some girls, but not for Daisy. She might marry me, but she'd hate me like poison ever after. And see how nice that would be when she got her money! No; I must tire her out, but I won't do as you say. Let's have a bit of supper now, and I'll think what's best to be done."

As Mrs. Foster kept her things in the front parlour Daisy thought it high time to go.

So she crept upstairs and into her room, where she locked herself in, and, throwing herself on the bed, indulged in a passion of tears.

This outburst and the quiet of the house, only disturbed by the dull murmer of voices, had their natural effect, and she fell presently into a heavy sleep.

How long she slept she knew not, but after a time she was awakened by a hot hand on her cold bare shoulder, shaking her to arouse her.

And, starting up, she saw Gedge Foote standing by the side of her bed.

His face wore a diabolical smile, and she could tell by the flush upon his hideous features that he had been drinking.

"I want to speak to you, Daisy," he said, in a thick voice.

"Why did you not send Mrs. Foster up, then, and I would have come down?" she said, striving to get away.

But this was not possible.

He had passed his arm round her waist, and was looking gloatingly upon her flushed face and her freely-displayed beauties — the white, dainty, girlish shoulders, and the budding bosom, now panting with angry excitement.

"Nay, I like you best thus, my pretty one," he said, bending down and kissing her pouting lips. "I shall not detain you long. Are you aware that your enemies are after you?"

"My enemies!" she cried. "Why should I have any?"

He laughed loudly.

"Why!" he cried. "You ask that? Was not your father murdered by your enemies because they feared he would prove his innocence and claim his property?"

"But my poor father is dead! Why should they persecute me?"

She was sitting quietly now, with her lovely head nearly resting on his chest, her white, dimpled shoulder touching his.

To resist him was, as she saw, utterly useless, and to cry out for help not only useless, but likely to bring upon her further disaster.

"Because you, as Herbert Leigh's daughter, are as dangerous as he was," said Gedge. "But I have sworn to protect you. You are

161

poor and friendless. I will be your banker and your friend. I will make you my wife, and with my very life I will protect you against the world.''

He could not but feel the shuddering thrill which invaded her form as he spoke, and it roused all his evil passions.

"Beware," he said, "how you insult me. I felt you tremble at my words."

"Can I help my feelings?" she said, meekly.

She thought it best to temporise.

"Nor can I help them," he said, and as if roused still more by her demure beauty he suddenly bent down and rained kisses on her lips, her neck, and her white, warm, shoulders.

Strengthened by her shame she sprang up suddenly and wrenched herself from his clutches, with the exception of the grasp he had upon her arm with his left hand.

As she did so she gave vent to a long, piercing shriek.

This was followed by another and another, which rang through the old house, and went echoing out over the marshy land towards the river.

The effect upon Gedge was alarming.

His eyes glowed like coals of fire, his veins stood out like whipcord on his brow — his face was fairly distorted with passion.

"You've raised the devil in me now," he cried, as he rushed upon her and clasped her once more round the waist, "and you must take the consequences."

Again and again she shrieked.

And as she did so she exerted all the strength of her lithe, round limbs to throw him off.

The struggle — the contact with her lovely, active frame — only served to inflame him the more, and as they both breathed hard in their struggles Daisy felt her strength rapidly giving way.

"Release me and I will listen to you quietly," she gasped.

He only laughed loudly, and kissed her.

And then, like an echo, came a terrible laugh from without. "Ha! ha! ha!"

The demon laugh of the mysterious apparition was new to Gedge Foote.

But it was hailed with joy by Daisy.

Poor, shrinking, ill-used Daisy! She seemed to recognise the fact that the awful being who was the terror of London was in some way or another her friend.

The sound gave her renewed strength, and the muscles of her strong arms stood out as she held Gedge for a moment away from her.

"Gedge, you're mad to-night," she cried, gaspingly, trying to smile. "Let me be quiet, and I'll listen to all you say. Perhaps even I'll give you a kiss if you're very good. There's a good Gedge: let's sit down and discuss the future."

But the demon himself seemed to have possessed the dwarf.

His eyes were red, his features were more than ever distorted, and he laughed again aloud as she uttered her words breathlessly, for her bosom was rising and falling in tumultuous panting after her exertions.

"A kiss? Bah! you've defied me, and that won't satisfy me now. I'll have a dozen!"

Again the loud demon laughter — "Ha! ha! ha!" and then a strange sound was heard in the wide chimney.

Gedge was so mad with rage and passion that he heard nothing.

But Daisy did, and the thought that her protector was near gave her superhuman strength.

Her limbs writhed like those of a wrestler as Gedge struggled with her; but, though she felt sure that the combat would end at last in her discomfiture if no help was near, she seemed to be full of hope that she would be able to hold out if this was really a champion coming to the rescue.

Almost at the instant that, with white, set face and panting breast, she felt that she could resist no more, there was a heavy fall down the chimney, something rolled out upon the floor, and with a wild and sepulchral laugh and a burst of sulphurous flame and smoke, Spring Heeled Jack stood before them.

Daisy in her present dilemma felt not the slightest fear of him.

But on Gedge the effect was electrical.

His hair seemed fairly to bristle on his head, his eyes appeared to start from their sockets, and his features worked convulsively.

He appeared as if striving to speak for a moment.

Then a wild, piercing shriek rent the air, and he fell prone on his face, striking his head violently against the fender.

As these strange cries and noises resounded through the house, it seemed wonderful that Mrs. Foster did not hurry up the stairs.

But she thought, of course, that the cries came from Daisy in her desperate struggles with Gedge Foote, and she purposely took no notice.

Daisy, meanwhile, trembling from head to foot, awed by the terrible aspect of the whole scene, afraid to look in the face of the awful apparition which had twice saved her, knelt at its feet, her eyes downcast, the long, silken waves of her hair veiling her bosom as she bent forward.

"How can I thank you, mysterious friend?" she said, in a low, gentle, quavering voice; "twice have you rescued me, first from the hands of an assassin, this time from a fate worse than death. I know not how, but some day I may be able to reward you."

There was no reply.

A strange stillness pervaded the room.

After a moment she looked up hurriedly, and a terrible faintness stole over her heart as she saw that the apparition had vanished.

A thick mist pervaded the room, a stifling sulphurous mist, which prevented her seeing much.

But, at any rate, she had heard and seen no movement, and she was alone with the senseless figure of Gedge Foote.

For a moment she stood leaning against the table in bewilderment.

The terrible scene which she had gone through, coupled with the apparition of Spring Heeled Jack, had for the time so shattered her nerves and bewildered her senses that she could not settle upon her course of action.

But with the first reawakening of her faculties she saw that unless something very miraculous occurred she was in no better position than before.

Gedge Foote would recover — he was only temporarily stunned — and after what had occurred he would be more desperate and furious than ever.

She could quit the room, but all the doors and windows below were bolted, and barred, and locked, and how, then, was she to escape?

Her first impulse, however, as soon as her strength began to return, was to put on her dress, hat, jacket, and boots.

Then, as she turned to the toilet table, she saw something which made her heart leap with joy.

It was a large bunch of keys.

Her eyes shone with pleasure, her bosom palpitated; for an instant she almost feared to clutch the keys for fear they should disappear before her eyes.

But at last she plucked up courage and seized them.

Then, with trembling limbs — more trembling because she saw that Gedge Foote showed signs of recovering — she made her way across the room, glided out, closed the door after her, locked it, and descended the stairs.

Where was Mrs. Foster?

Not a sound could she hear at first.

Then a loud snoring assailed her ears, and in order to be sure and prepared for any contingency she approached the back parlour and peered in.

164

The sight within would at any other time have excited her merriment.

Mrs. Foster was reclining in an arm-chair in a drunken sleep, her arms hanging helplessly by her side, her eyes only half shut, her face flushed, her mouth wide open, her toes cocked up helplessly.

But Daisy did not remain a moment.

Creeping out again she approached the front door, and as quickly as possible began to remove the bolts and bars.

Then she fitted a key to the lock, and, to her joy, opened it.

As she did so she heard a heavy stumbling noise upstairs, and Gedge Foote came heavily across the room, and began to try and force the lock.

He had recovered swiftly after she quitted the chamber; and now, finding himself in the dark and locked in, he began kicking and shouting to such an extent that he succeeded in awakening Mrs. Foster, who began to mumble vaguely and stumble about.

But by this time Daisy had succeeded in running out.

Shutting the door as softly as she could she ran along the little garden, and without thinking which way she was going scaled the fence opposite, and hurried across the marsh land towards the river.

The only guide she had was a small trembling light, which she had often seen from her window, and which she therefore knew must be a fixture belonging to some riverside cottage or landing place.

The way she had come, however, was a rough and difficult one.

Fearful every moment of pursuit she endeavoured to rush quickly on, but the ground was full of holes and ruts, and every now and then she sank above her ankles in the cloddy soil.

As she toiled slowly on she became aware of sounds behind her, and looking back, she saw someone pursuing her with a lantern.

It must be Gedge Foote.

The idea gave wings to Daisy's feet.

She had so lately escaped from desperate peril that her heart gave a great leap of annoyance and disgust at the very notion of being once more in his power, even for a moment.

Perilous and rugged as was the road, therefore, she hastened on.

Gedge, however, knew his way better than she did, and was able to make more rapid progress.

She soon saw this, and glanced round in every direction in search of some spot which would afford her temporary shelter.

But with the exception of a few stunted trees and so forth

there was nothing.

She must go on trusting to her fleetness of foot and quickness of eye.

On, on she went, now falling on her hands, now going ankle deep in the slush and mud, cutting her palms and bruising her soft little knees against the hard stones.

But she was resolute.

Anything was better than falling again into the power of her pretended friend, the one who had so basely betrayed her.

She cared not for cuts and bruises as long as she was able to put a good distance between herself and pursuer.

The attempt, however, seemed vain.

Gedge Foote came on nearer and nearer.

As she was now not far from the river, she could see that the light she had before noticed was on a barge anchored close to the bank.

If she could but reach this!

Panting for breath, her heart beating rebelliously in her swelling bosom, she made one final effort.

The ground, however, became more rugged.

Gedge Foote was close behind her, she could hear his hard breathing; she seemed almost able to feel his clutching hands.

She knew now that wherever he caught her he would have no mercy.

And so, sick at heart at the prospect of losing home, and perhaps life itself, out on that desolate waste land, she gave one long shrill shriek for help, and made one more desperate struggle.

"Ha! ha! ha!

What was that?

A loud demon laugh, a whirring sound of wings, a stump, stump, stump, as of some strange leaping animal.

And then a wild shriek from Gedge Foote, as the terrible apparition of Spring Heeled Jack sprang between him and his victim.

To Daisy the awful sight was associated with safety.

And so, although she had no desire to pause in its presence, she made no exclamation of fear, but dashed away as quickly as possible towards the river.

Gedge Foote had fallen into a deep hole, and there for a few moments he remained crouching, with his hands over his eyes.

Then, as all seemed quiet, he ventured to remove his hands, and look up.

But Spring Heeled Jack was not gone.

He was still near at hand, standing on a mound, a weird and spectral figure in the grey light, and smoke and flame issuing from his mouth.

"She has escaped me now by the devil's aid," he said; "but she shall not escape me always. Let her go now. I shall soon be on her track again!"

But at this the terrible figure's laughter rang out once again in challenging tones.

"Ha! ha! ha!"

Acknowledgements

During the years in which I have been investigating the legend of Spring Heeled Jack many people have helped me with pieces of information and suggestions and I regret they are obviously too numerous to mention. However, I should particularly like to thank the following who have been generous with their time and advice while the book itself was being written: David Philips who, as so often before, 'sprang' the goods when they were needed; Denis Gifford who knows nearly everything there is to know about comics and films; Peter Stephens of the *News of the World*; Raymond Mander and Joe Mitchenson of the Mander & Mitchenson Theatre Collection; the staffs of the British Museum and the London Library; Reg Smith of the *Illustrated London News*; Eileen Buckle and Timothy Good of FSR Publications; Miss Roberta Routledge of Routledge Associates; The British Film Institute; and the publishers of *The Times*, *The Daily Telegraph*, *The Daily Mail*, *The Evening News*, *Notes & Queries* and *Flying Saucer Review*. Finally Anne Williams for her enthusiasm over the project and Pamela Scott for efficiently typing the manuscript.

Index